BLOWING

ON THE

CHANGES

BLOWING

ON THE

LESLIE GOURSE

CHANGES

The Art of the Jazz Horn Players

FRANKLIN WATTS

A Division of Grolier Publishing
New York / London / Hong Kong / Sydney
Danbury, Connecticut

For Editor E. Russell Primm III
with special thanks for his support

Designed by John D. Sparks
Jacket Illustration by Robert Hanewich

Photographs ©: AP/Wide World Photos: 92, 95, 105 bottom; Corbis-Bettmann: 89 top; Frank Driggs
Collection: 22, 42 bottom, 51 top, 55, 59, 63 top, 73 left, 90, 91, 105 top, 110 bottom, 120;
Penguin/Corbis-Bettmann: 89 bottom; Retna Ltd./William P. Gottlieb: 63 bottom; UPI/Corbis-
Bettmann: 87, 93, 94; William P. Gottlieb, Library of Congress: Ira & Leonore S. Gershwin Fund:
32, 42 top, 51 bottom, 73 right, 78, 84, 85, 86, 88, 99, 110 top.

Library of Congress Cataloging-in-Publication Data

Gourse, Leslie.
Blowing on the Changes: The Art of the Jazz Horn Players / by Leslie Gourse.

p.   cm. — (The Art of Jazz)
Discography: p.
Includes bibliographical references and index.
Contents: Louis "Pops" Armstrong blows on the changes — Louis Armstrong thrills and influences
his whole generation — Other great Swing Era horn players — More great reed and brass players in
the big bands — Dizzy Gillespie, Charlie "Bird" Parker, and the bebop revolution — The orbit of
Miles Davis — Other important horn players of the 1950s and 1960s — John Coltrane and Eric
Dolphy — Ornette Coleman, free jazz, and jazz-rock fusion — A jazz renaissance.
ISBN 0-531-11357-4 (lib. bdg.)   0-531-15880-2 (pbk.)
1. Jazz musicians — United States — Biography. 2. Wind instrument players — United States —
Biography. 3. Jazz — History and criticism. I. Title. II. Series.
ML399.G66   1997
788'.165'0922 — dc21
[B]   96–50938
                                                                      CIP
                                                                    AC MN

CONTENTS

INTRODUCTION

THE POPULARITY OF THE JAZZ HORN PLAYERS

In the jazz world, all the instrumentalists are important, but the horn players usually get the most attention. The phrase "young man with a horn" has always been used to symbolize the glamour of jazz musicians; a 1950 movie with that title was based on the life story of cornetist Bix Beiderbecke, whose bright sound in the early years of jazz alerted all the trumpet players—and other instrumentalists, too. Horn players often lead groups. And of all the people who play horns, the trumpeters and the alto and tenor saxophonists usually get the loudest, longest cheers.

In the renaissance of jazz that took place in the 1980s and 1990s, jazz trumpeters became the most popular players. Whenever gifted trumpeters showed up, the critics and audiences flocked to hear them. It was especially exciting one night in 1991 in Bradley's, a Manhattan jazz club, when Freddie Hubbard, a fifty-three-year-old trumpeter who had been a charismatic star for many years, came to listen to a new player, Roy Hargrove.

Small, wiry, and only twenty-one years old, Roy had already become well known for his loud, intense, fiery style. He had been practicing day and night to learn the skills and style of the legendary, veteran trumpeters. (Both his parents worked on night shifts in the Texas city where he grew up. An only child, he used to fill up the quietness of the nights by practicing his trumpet.) The trumpeters best known to the public were Louis ("Pops") Armstrong, Dizzy Gillespie, and Miles Davis.

Roy's practice had paid off. He began starring in clubs and festivals in his teen years. By his twenties, he was touring around the world, especially Europe and Japan, where he led his own groups.

So the crowd at Bradley's buzzed. Freddie Hubbard shouted encouragement to Roy. The pianist in the group, John Hicks, himself a dazzling, older player, rose to introduce Roy. He stood up at the microphone and said, "Let's have a big round of applause for Louis Armstrong. We all knew he would come back, but we didn't know when."

No star in the jazz world has ever shone more brightly than "Pops" Armstrong. In the 1920s, he created the foundation of modern jazz by improvising on the chords of written songs with his warm, full sound. Dizzy Gillespie and Miles Davis, who built on Pops's innovations and broadened the art and scope of jazz, approached the founder's fame.

Only alto saxophonist Charlie "Bird" Parker earned more credit in jazz circles in the 1940s and 1950s than his trumpet-playing peers. Bird was the greatest innovator on any instrument after Pops. Before Bird, tenor saxophonist Coleman Hawkins became idolized for his extraordinary, big sound. He played long, beautiful lines, which listeners called a fluid style.

Neither the saxophone nor the trumpet was regarded as a first-rate instrument in the classical music world. Armstrong and Hawkins explored the potential of their instruments and set high standards. They even influenced trumpet and saxophone techniques in the classical music world. In the 1960s, tenor and soprano saxophone player John Coltrane extended the innovations of all the previous saxophonists (particularly Charlie Parker, who was the most progressive of Coltrane's predecessors) by improvising in more daring ways. "'Trane," as he was called, played with Miles Davis's group in the 1950s.

Miles liberated his group, including 'Trane, from the tyranny of the constant flow of chord changes that had developed in the bebop style. Miles's men improvised from modes and tonal centers instead. Thoroughly schooled by Miles, 'Trane also worked with the great bebop pianist and composer Thelonious Monk. In Monk's group, Coltrane learned more about harmonies, timing, and space from a master. In 1959, 'Trane began leading his own groups, and with them, between 1960 and 1965, he demonstrated a great, dark, spiritually throbbing technique and tone in his dense tapestry of music. He seemed to play a million notes— "sheets of sound," critic Ira Gitler called it.[1] As another tenor saxophonist, Jimmy Heath, described 'Trane's style, he "looped" around the way a very fast-fingered pianist could.[2]

Coltrane progressed from composing modal music to free jazz— music completely free of chords. His technique, compositions, and spirituality made him the most influential modern saxophonist. Many young saxophonists decided to commit themselves to their instruments once they heard 'Trane's exciting music. Then they also studied Lester Young, Coleman Hawkins, Charlie Parker, and the others who had helped 'Trane build his technique and formulate creative ideas.

At first, Coltrane played alto saxophone, but he switched to tenor to escape the dominance of Charlie Parker on the alto and explore the deeper, darker-voiced tenor sax. Bird's creative imagination and the artistic beauty of his compositions were so influential that, during his lifetime and for decades after his death in 1955, more young musicians than ever before decided to play the alto.

By 1980, however, trumpeters were again causing the most excitement. The most famous was Wynton Marsalis, a clean-cut, soft-spoken musician, who wore little round eyeglasses and fashionable suits. He looked like a banker, talked with the self-possession of a prime minister, and played trumpet like an angel.

Columbia Records signed Marsalis to contracts in 1981, when he was about nineteen years old, to make both classical and jazz recordings. The public loved him. He was one of the main reasons for a renewed interest in jazz in the 1980s. When he became famous, he felt a great responsibility to educate the public about the glories of jazz. One of his greatest accomplishments was to establish jazz as a constituent art at New York's Lincoln Center, which regularly presents jazz concerts, films, and lectures. Never before had jazz been accorded such respect.

Wynton leads the official Lincoln Center Jazz Orchestra. At the same time, trumpeter Jon Faddis, Dizzy Gillespie's protégé, leads the new jazz program at Carnegie Hall and its official band. So the two most prestigious jazz bands in the country are headed by the two most famous young jazz trumpeters.

Another of Wynton's great achievements at Lincoln Center was to conduct a new Young People's Jazz concert series to teach schoolchildren the history of jazz. As a member of jazz drummer Art Blakey's band in the early 1980s, Wynton Marsalis had played flashy hard bop in the rococo tradition handed down by Bird. That is, Wynton had played a great deal of improvisation with a blues-rooted feeling. After he left Blakey, Wynton went on to play in all the jazz styles; he especially concentrated on the music originated by Pops Armstrong and Duke Ellington during the swing era in the early part of the century.

But Wynton (not to mention Pops, Dizzy, and Miles) is not the only reason that so many popular jazz players are trumpeters. Musicians salute the carrying power and loudness of the trumpet. Pitched in the register of the human cry, the trumpet can cut through nearly every other sound. "The trumpet is the clarion. The instrument speaks with majesty," explains Wynton. "When the trumpeter plays, there's always some heroics taking place."[3]

This most serious of players puts forth the not-so-serious theory that players of this attention-getting instrument "are crazy. They're the ones who are always cutting up in the back of the band and getting into trouble." His comment calls to mind an incident in 1940 when someone threw a spitball at bandleader Cab Calloway. Even though Dizzy Gillespie, then in Cab's trumpet section, hadn't thrown it, he got the blame. He and Cab got into a terrible fight, and it took them a few years to make up. (By then, Cab had learned who really threw the spitball—Jonah Jones, another trumpeter.)

Roy Hargrove offers a theory about the reason for the trumpet's popularity: "Trumpeters who establish themselves usually become leaders. It's an instrument that tends to lead."[4] The leadership quality that prompts a person to stick with the trumpet also explains its dominance. "You have to have an aggressive personality just to produce tones in different registers on this instrument," says Terence Blanchard, a trumpeter who was thirty-two years old in 1995. His star rose in the 1980s after Wynton became famous. In addition to conventional engagements in clubs and concerts, Terence began playing and writing music for Spike Lee's movies and other film projects. (In the 1980s, Lee won fame as a filmmaker, telling serious stories about African-Americans.) "Everything on the trumpet is determined by wind," says Terence, "and the force it takes may manifest itself in some people's personalities."[5] Wynton Marsalis agrees with Terence. "It's an ornery instrument. You have to manhandle it."

Miles Davis, who appeared to be an introvert and had difficulty talking to people, exhibited drive, flamboyance, and adventurousness in his trumpet playing. The trumpet's role as leader goes back to the Bible, "to Gabriel! to God and fanfare!" explains Freddie Hubbard.[6] (Actually, Gabriel never played trumpet in the St. James version of the Bible. And the trumpet as we know it didn't exist in biblical times. And other angels played horns. But Gabriel got all the credit.)

Dr. Donald Byrd, a jazz professor and trumpeter, teaches that Africans played forerunners of the trumpet, as did the Roman heralds. Horns existed in various forms during the Middle Ages. Baroque-era composers wrote for an unkeyed version of the trumpet before the invention of valves made it a reliable instrument to include in orchestras.

Still, when the trumpet wasn't being sounded on battlefields or at royal coronations of kings and queens, its primary function in orchestral music was to supply dynamics—loudness in ensemble passages. Trumpeters weren't soloists. As recently as 1921, a classical cornetist, Herbert L. Clarke, advised a younger player to abandon the trumpet because of its "cutting sound and loudness," says Jon Faddis, a master of the trumpet's highest register. Clarke insisted that the instrument was only good for jazz, "which is either the nearest hell or the devil's music."[7]

Clarke was a lousy prophet, for along came Louis Armstrong. With his outgoing personality and creative genius, he inspired jazz trumpeters and cornetists to turn themselves into virtuosos. Armstrong played cornet, a trumpet-like instrument, and then switched to the trumpet in the mid-1920s. After World War II, trumpet soloists became more prominent in European classical music, too, thanks to the masterful classical player Maurice André and a few others.

Long gone are the days early in the twentieth century when aspiring trumpeters jammed on street corners in New Orleans to see who could play loudest. Back then, everyone listened to records to copy Armstrong's technique—his slurs, phrasing, rhythms, harmonies, and melodies. By the late 1960s, music schools and colleges brought jazz into their curricula, prompted by the civil rights movement, equal opportunity laws, and the subsequent recognition of African-American culture in academic circles.

Jazz musicians today study their art formally. They learn music theory, jazz history, composition, arranging, and performance techniques for playing in big and small groups. Technology, too, has done its share to promote trumpeters. Miles Davis used amplification to make sure his haunting, eerie sound with its center of gravity in the trumpet's middle register—not its high one—could be heard in the midst of his very loud fusion jazz groups. These groups combined acoustic and electric instruments.

Wynton Marsalis came of age in an era when compact discs enticed young people to buy sophisticated audio equipment. In a high-tech age,

Wynton's artistic and commercial successes sold CDs by the hundreds of thousands. Happy record company executives then signed other youngsters in a search for more Wyntons.

Many of these new talents played other instruments. They recognized the trumpet's assertiveness and knew they could get a lot of attention by playing it. But they had other priorities. "The popularity of the trumpet has crossed my mind," admitted alto saxophonist Vincent Herring, who was thirty-two in 1995. "But I love the soft sound of the alto saxophone."[8]

Even trumpet players are daunted by the instrument's legacy. Terence Blanchard was upset by the idea that trumpeters had to lead and have their own characteristic sounds, ideas, and styles. He used to go around brooding, "I've got to find my direction." Dizzy Gillespie, who always loved to help young musicians, laughed when he heard Terence's lament. Terence recalls Dizzy telling him, " 'You don't wear the same clothes as other people, and you walk your own way. So just play, and you'll have your direction.' " From Dizzy, Terence learned the liberating lesson that what a musician communicates honestly and naturally on any instrument can make him or her distinguished.

Probably the greatest threat to the leadership of the trumpet is the saxophone. Saxophonists and trumpeters have always carried on a sweet competition in the jazz world. During the swing era, the most important jazz saxophonists played tenor. Don Byas, Ben Webster, Lester Young, and Coleman Hawkins, four of the most respected musicians in jazz history, played tenor. Their styles affected every other saxophonist, as well as musicians on many other instruments.

There were many other stirring tenor players in those early days of jazz, too. Herschel Evans, who died young, Ike Quebec, Paul Quinichette, and Paul Gonsalves played in bands led by Count Basie, Duke Ellington, and Cab Calloway. Many great saxophonists played in Woody Herman's band, called the Thundering Herd, including a famed quartet dubbed the Four Brothers. In the big-band era of the 1930s and 1940s, people formed fan clubs for their favorite saxophonists, many of whom led their own bands. And if one powerful saxophonist, playing in a section as a sideman, left a band, the group's whole sound changed.

In the 1930s, Lester Young developed a soft-toned, fluid style. His originality heralded the coming revolution of progressive jazz, which would be called bebop. Coleman Hawkins, called "King of the Tenor Saxophone," had a loud and haunting sound. In 1938, he made a classic recording of "Body and Soul." Nobody has ever played it better.

Other single-reed players—baritone and soprano saxophonists and clarinetists—have had important roles in jazz, too. Two of the greatest swing-era bandleaders, Artie Shaw and Benny Goodman, played clarinet. The high-pitched sound of the clarinet would fall out of favor during the bebop era with its more aggressive sound. The tenorists of the swing era, and the altoists, after Charlie Parker in the 1940s, have turned out to be the ones to stand shoulder to shoulder with the trumpeters in the esteem and affection of audiences. From the 1940s into the 1980s, some people even thought that saxophonists were the most glamorous jazz musicians, particularly because of Charlie Parker and John Coltrane. The competition for leadership still goes on between the saxophonists and trumpeters.

Occasionally other horn players distinguish themselves as charismatic jazz masters. The trombone is the second most popular brass instrument in jazz. One of the best-known musicians among the jazz pioneers in the early part of the twentieth century was bandleader/trombonist Edward "Kid" Ory from New Orleans. Swing-era bandleader Tommy Dorsey, Jack Teagarden, who led his own group and played with Louis Armstrong, and Joe "Tricky Sam" Nanton and Juan Tizol from Duke Ellington's band all became role models in their day. Some famous modern players include Slide Hampton, Al Grey, Benny Powell, the bebop innovator J. J. Johnson, female arranger and player Melba Liston, and a younger player named Steve Turre.

Soprano and baritone saxophonists have dominated groups, too. Sidney Bechet of New Orleans played soprano sax. He was hailed as a

14

genius in England and went to live in France, where he became a super-star in the first half of the twentieth century. In recent years, a pop-jazz star, Kenny G, who wears his hair in a long, shaggy style, has become rich and famous for his shrill style on the soprano. Jazz experts don't like his music, but the public loves it. Wayne Shorter, who played tenor with Miles Davis's band in the 1960s, has also become popular as a soprano saxophonist and a composer.

Several baritone saxophonists have built forceful reputations for their virtuosity—Harry Carney with Duke Ellington's early band, Gerry Mulligan, Charles Davis, British player John Surman, Howard Johnson (who also plays tuba), Joe Temperley (a Welshman who came to the United States and played with Duke Ellington's band), and journeyman Danny Banks. Audiences beg Temperley, with his smooth, fluid, haunting style, to play encores.

Many alto and tenor saxophonists double on other instruments. Frank Wess, who started his career in the 1950s with Count Basie's band, plays flute as well as he does alto and tenor. James Moody, hired by Dizzy Gillespie in 1948 during the heyday of early bebop, plays flute and saxophones masterfully. Some flutists play only flutes, but jazz flutists find much more work if they play saxophones, too. Saxophonists often double these days on clarinets, too, including the mellow-pitched bass clarinet.

Many types of brass and reed instruments have been used in jazz. Brass instruments include the fluegelhorn (which produces a softer tone than the trumpet), tuba, euphonium (which looks like a little tuba and is to the trombone what the fluegelhorn is to the trumpet), and French horn. In the jazz world today, trumpets, trombones, and fluegelhorns are the most popular brass instruments. French horns are sometimes used. The tuba, which can play in the same deep register as the bass fiddle, was very popular in early jazz; it occasionally has a role in big groups today. The reed instruments most popular in jazz are all single reeds (they use a single wooden reed attached to a plastic or metal mouthpiece)—saxophones and clarinets. Double-reed woodwinds, such as oboes and bassoons, remain primarily in the classical music world.

ONE

LOUIS "POPS" ARMSTRONG BLOWS ON THE CHANGES

The person often credited with inventing jazz and helping to popularize swing was a New Orleans-born trumpeter, Louis Armstrong, called "Pops" for his genius as a jazz innovator.

New Orleans is a beautiful, warm port city with a Caribbean ambiance at the mouth of the muddy, churning Mississippi River. The Spanish ruled the city at the end of the eighteenth century. Emperor Napoléon Bonaparte, France's great military leader, took it over for France and then sold it to the United States in 1803 in the Louisiana Purchase. Boats with all sorts of goods and people with different backgrounds were always coming and going. They made New Orleans a booming port in the nineteenth century.

Different cultures and races blended there—whites from many countries, descendants of former African slaves, and American Indians. French-speaking Cajuns migrated from Canada to the swampy bayou country near New Orleans, and West Indians moved north to the city. People of color mingled more freely with whites in nineteenth-century New Orleans than they did in the rest of the South. A subgroup called Creoles—generally, those of mixed French, Spanish, or African descent—emerged as a unique cultural group in the U.S. Gulf states.

Wealthy white fathers with talented Creole children often sent the children to Paris to study music. But in the 1890s, segregation became the law in parts of the United States. Creoles of mixed race were demoted in status in New Orleans. By law there, life became meaner for African-Americans or anyone with even a small percentage of African heritage.

The multicultural citizens of New Orleans didn't want to end their freewheeling lifestyle completely. The sultry, humid weather, the artistic, elaborate French architecture with its wrought-iron latticework, and the Mississippi River all added to the sensual, even mysterious atmosphere of the city. Many people headed for Storyville, an area of the city divided into white and African-American sections and filled with honky-tonks, bars, clubs, and brothels. Some places were well known as "black and tans," where African-Americans and whites socialized, danced, drank, sang, and played the blues and other popular music of the day. Gamblers and others who lived by their wits indulged in the pleasures of the flesh and in petty crimes. Police were supposed to enforce segregation and other laws, but club owners often paid them to look the other way.

Holidays that were celebrated for a day in other cities often lasted a week in New Orleans. People liked to join private associations or clubs that sponsored parties. Every weekend, club members staged picnics along the Mississippi River or Lake Pontchartrain, which bounded the city. People brought plenty to eat and drink, threw sawdust on the ground, and danced all night. They hired little bands to provide the music. Musicians often received their pay in hot dogs and drinks. After work on Fridays, everybody went out "good-timing" some place in town, and they didn't go back to their jobs until after "Blue Monday" was over.

African-American musicians traveled around town in trucks, singing and playing in different neighborhoods. They passed a hat to collect tips as payment. Talented children formed sidewalk quartets and sang and danced for passersby. Even funerals in New Orleans were jubilant celebrations.

When someone died, especially a man whom other people liked or respected, he was treated to a genuine New Orleans funeral. He was placed in a coffin on a carriage drawn by white horses. His fellow club members dressed up in their uniforms and hired a band to march with them. The band played a sad, slow dirge as it followed the mourners and the coffin all the way to the cemetery. Popular songs for funerals were "Jesus, Lover of My Soul" and "Nearer My God to Thee." After the dead person was buried, the mourners headed back to town.

On the way home, the band speeded up the tempo of the music and played joyful songs in a two-beat rhythm. People clapped their hands to that steady, syncopated beat. "When the Saints Go Marching In" was a favorite hymn. The New Orleans style made it a happy music to help the mourners get over their sorrow. This funeral music represented the spirit of the city.

The tradition, which began in the nineteenth century, still exists today. Not only does a band play, but strangers who never knew the dead person join in. They dance and play instruments, too, and are called the "Second Line." The whole funeral procession has come to be known familiarly as the Second Line.

Budding young musicians have always felt lucky to grow up in New Orleans. Some became well known for the New Orleans spirit and style of music. Among them were cornetists Charles "Buddy" Bolden and Bunk Johnson, both born in the late nineteenth century. Both men lived wild lives. Buddy played so loudly and excitingly that people said they could hear him play clear across the Mississippi River. He could also play sweet waltzes and ballads. But he became ill by 1906, probably from alcohol, and by 1907 he was living in a mental hospital.

Bunk Johnson won fame for his playing. Like Buddy, Bunk had a weakness for alcohol. In the 1940s, jazz historians found him working in the fields down south and brought him to recording studios in the north, where they recorded him along with New Orleans musicians who had worked steadily and built careers. But Bunk kept drinking, and it was impossible to revive his career.

Other New Orleans musicians were influenced by the creative, spirited music of these early jazz cornetists, such as trombonist Kid Ory, who led the best band in New Orleans, and cornetist Freddie Keppard. Both of them employed a popular cornetist named Joe "King" Oliver. "Baby" Dodds, a drummer, his brother, clarinetist Johnny Dodds, and another clarinetist named Jimmie Noone became adept at playing swinging, two-beat, New Orleans-style music with creative embellishments. All of them had so much drive that they eventually left New Orleans and spread the sound of early jazz to Chicago, the West Coast, and New York. Other talented musicians may have played in the early jazz style in other cities, but the New Orleans "cats" made recordings, which made them well known throughout the world.

It was in the high-spirited, music-oriented culture of New Orleans that Louis Armstrong was born to a very poor African-American family on August 4, 1901 — "from the bottom of the well, one step from hell," the saying went.[1] He heard music every day: gospel hymns in the churches, Second Line funeral bands, blues in the honky-tonks near his home, Cajun music played with accordions, violins, and percussion, African-derived drumming rituals, the two-beat syncopated music that developed from a blend of African traditions and European harmonies, music from minstrel shows and vaudeville theaters, the music of classically-trained Creole and white musicians, the haunting Spanish-influenced melodies brought to town by visitors from Caribbean countries, and bands at lakeside parties on weekends.

Before he was ten, Louis began singing the soprano part with a sidewalk quartet of little boys. He claimed he had heard Buddy Bolden play in New Orleans and didn't like Bolden's rough, loud sound. But Louis was only six when Bolden went to a hospital, and so it's unlikely he heard Bolden play. Louis certainly heard about him, however, from Joe Oliver and other older musicians.

Louis's mother, Mayann, had migrated from the countryside to New Orleans. Louis loved to listen to music played in the honky-tonks near the single room where he lived with his mother and sister nicknamed Mama Lucy. Louis's father had left Mayann for another woman and started another family. Too young to go into the honky-tonks, Louis peeked through chinks in the walls and watched the blues singers dancing with customers. He especially adored cornet players. For his own sidewalk quartet, he thought he might attract more attention and tips if he played a whistle; so he bought one.

He was working with his quartet downtown one New Year's Eve when everybody, including Louis, felt like celebrating. He heard a boy across the street fire a pistol into the air. Though it was illegal, people in New Orleans would do this on holidays. Louis had borrowed a pistol belonging to one of his mother's boyfriends and fired it to show off to his friends and join in the noisy celebration.

Suddenly a white policeman grabbed him. Louis begged not to be arrested, but the policeman locked him up. At dawn, a judge decided Louis was a wayward boy and sentenced him for an indefinite period to the Colored Waifs' Home for Boys on the edge of town. For the first three days, he missed his family so much that he didn't eat.

Trying to adjust to school, he decided to join its band. The bandmaster let him try a cornet. Louis practiced constantly and became so good that he was appointed bandleader. That was an important step for him. The school helped to support itself with the earnings of its student band, which traveled on a truck and entertained in different neighborhoods in New Orleans. When the band went to Storyville, Louis's mother and all her neighbors came out to hear him play. He was wearing a brown- and cream-colored uniform that he loved. He felt proud that his neighbors, poor as they were (and some of them gamblers and petty thieves), donated big tips to the band.

Louis impressed older musicians who heard him playing cornet around town. Sidney Bechet sometimes played in a band with Louis that traveled by truck around New Orleans. Bechet came from a family filled

Louis Armstrong is in the middle in this 1923 photograph of Joe "King" Oliver's Creole Jazz Band in Chicago. Oliver is to his left, and Lil Hardin is at the piano.

with talented musicians, and so he was used to hearing good music. He thought Louis played very well and with an exceptionally strong sound. In fact, the two youngsters actually competed with each other.

When Louis left the Colored Waifs' Home, Joe Oliver and other musicians advised him about technique and hired him for their bands, which played on trucks, at picnics, in honky-tonks, and in funerals. Oliver gave Louis a new cornet to replace a banged-up instrument he had bought in a pawn shop. Oliver and his wife also invited Louis to dinner and served him his favorite food, red beans and rice, a popular "soul food" in New Orleans.

Joe Oliver went up the Mississippi River to St. Louis on a boat, then traveled by train to Chicago, where he formed his own band, becoming known as "King" Oliver. Kid Ory invited Louis to take Oliver's place in the best band in New Orleans. A fine New Orleans banjo and guitar player named Danny Barker, eight years younger than Louis, had strong memories of how well Armstrong learned to play his cornet: "He came out of the Colored Waifs' Home for Boys, blowing sounds that no one had ever heard before."[2]

Later, when Louis, too, went to live in Chicago, he switched to trumpet. It was similar to the cornet but had a sharper, more brilliant sound. And he kept developing his unique style based on the music he already knew. By embellishing everything he heard in New Orleans, and making his blend swing with Dixieland's characteristic two-beat rhythm, he was creating the foundation of modern jazz.

He sang in exactly the same style with which he played his horn. Every singer and instrumentalist who came along after him would look up to him as the originator of a new style. Danny Barker knew all about Louis's musical influences and education. Louis had heard scat singing, songs without words, "monkey-shine singing," as Danny said it was called. He believed it came from the Cajuns in the bayous. Louis also paid special attention in the early 1920s to recordings by the early blues and popular singers when they played at the Lyric Theater in New Orleans or simply entertained in the streets and the joints.

Louis also liked the way the ragtime piano players treated music, playing all the notes in a chord. He started playing them, too, instead of just the one note that the cornetist or trumpeter was supposed to play. And he also played notes that the chords suggested to him—notes that fit in well with the written chords. That is, he improvised. Musicians called the technique "blowing on the changes." (Chords were referred to as "changes" because they progressed from one to the next, and also because the notes of the chords could be changed.) And sometimes the improvising led to the invention of a new melody—harmonic variation was built on the harmonic progression or outline (the chord changes) of the original theme.[3] This is partly how he created modern jazz. He bent the notes, gliding from one to another, for a deeper, more plaintive, emotionally stirring sound. That technique followed the African-American tradition—the way people sang in churches.

"Most trumpet players were playing staccato," explained Danny Barker. "Louis Armstrong began playing legato and soaring on the notes with long phrases. He sang the same way. To see him in person was exhilarating. He scooped up everything he had ever heard in Storyville and every place else and put it together."

In 1922, King Oliver invited Louis to join his group in an African-American neighborhood on the South Side of Chicago. By then Louis was twenty-one years old. (He claimed that he had been born on July 4, 1900, but he was actually born in 1901; he wanted to get a draft card and present himself as a little older than he was, especially when he searched for jobs.[4]) King Oliver had actually invited Armstrong before 1922, but Louis had hesitated. He had been happy working in New Orleans and on the riverboats that traveled on the Mississippi River up to St. Louis and back. And he had fallen in love with and married a prostitute named Daisy, who worked in honky-tonks. It wasn't really shocking for Louis to marry her. In those days, he mingled all the time with tough characters in Storyville. He himself never took part in criminal activities, because he loved his horn. He knew his love for music was his saving grace.

By 1922, however, he and Daisy were fighting so much that he felt he had to get away from her. His mother escorted him to the boat to say good-bye and gave him a fish sandwich to begin his journey to join King Oliver in Chicago. Farther up the country, he switched to a train. King Oliver went to the station to meet Louis, but the train was late. Oliver had to hurry to the Lincoln Gardens where he was leading his Creole Jazz Band. Louis made his way there alone. Standing outside the club, he felt intimidated by the sight of Chicago's big buildings, the fast pace of the street traffic, and the sound of the band swinging inside. He nearly turned around to catch a train back to New Orleans. But he stepped inside the club for a minute. King Oliver was delighted to see him. Louis felt safe, and he stayed in Chicago.

TWO

LOUIS ARMSTRONG THRILLS AND INFLUENCES HIS WHOLE GENERATION

*T*he 1920s were a revolutionary time for musicians and singers, with the improvement of amplification and recording techniques and mass-produced recordings. Armstrong made records with blues singers and with King Oliver's band. He met a woman named Lil Hardin, a pianist, who encouraged and advised him about how to manage his budding career. His marriage to Daisy was over, so Louis and Lil married. From his recordings, musicians everywhere got a chance to hear his thrilling style and tone on trumpet. A white singer named Al Jolson, a superstar in the 1920s and 1930s, heard Armstrong's records. And Bing Crosby, who would become one of the country's best and most popular singers, revered Jolson's style. So indirectly, Bing felt Louis's influence even before he heard Louis in person in Chicago in the 1920s.

Louis was then most in demand for his trumpet playing. Lil encouraged him to go to work in New York, where he made a hit in 1924 playing with a highly respected African-American band led by Fletcher Henderson. By that time, Louis wanted to stop working in Oliver's shadow. He was playing obbligato and accompaniment behind Oliver instead of soloing and showing off his own gifts. Fletcher Henderson's band had become popular at the Roseland Ballroom in midtown New York. Henderson wanted to give his band as much pizzazz as possible in order to compete with another popular band led by Paul Whiteman. Louis was exactly what Henderson needed.

Louis had come out of the tradition of New Orleans jazz that included collective improvisation. All the musicians in a group agreed upon what song they were playing. Then they improvised together so that they complemented each other without duplicating musical parts. Pops had such technical mastery, great musical form, and creative imagination that he became an exciting soloist. He didn't want to submerge himself in the collective sound of a group. Instead he used the group as a foil for his own playing out front. It was in this setting that he developed improvisation as a new composition based on the harmonic structure of the original song. He was also developing his masterful blues tonality.

Black and white audiences at the Roseland Ballroom called out for the exciting trumpeter to solo. He also electrified Harlem audiences when he played with Henderson at the Lafayette Theater in 1925, appearing on the same bill with many prominent Harlem musicians. Even so, he decided to return to Chicago and work in the orchestra pit at the Vendome Theater for Erskine Tate and his New Orleans band. Crowds flocked there to hear Louis play countless high Cs at every performance. Sometimes he played so hard that his top lip bled by the end of the night.

Another trumpeter, Adolphus "Doc" Cheatham, born in Nashville, Tennessee, and steeped in early swing-era jazz with strong New Orleans roots, was working in the Dreamland Café on Chicago's South Side in the 1920s. One day Louis walked in the door and asked Doc to substitute for him at the Vendome. He had a special reason for going to Cheatham. New Orleans musicians were the most famous, and fame had gone to their heads. They were jealous of the peerless Armstrong. Nobody could outplay him, but he didn't like the disrespectful treatment they gave him. So for a sub, he chose Doc, a stranger who wasn't so competitive.

"And Tate was as mean as he could be," Doc recalled about the orchestra leader many years later. "Neither Tate nor any of the other musicians in that band said anything to me. And Tate for meanness rehearsed the specialty and did the solo on 'Poor Little Rich Girl,' Armstrong's feature. I did it my own way. Nobody said one word of encouragement. The night of the show, people were screaming and applauding. When the spotlight hit me, the applause stopped. The people were expecting Armstrong." Doc got $80 for that show and did it once again at Armstrong's request.[1]

Many young musicians were totally bowled over by Louis's technique and feeling. A schoolboy named Jonah Jones was about to quit playing music when he went to Chicago from his native Louisville, Kentucky, on an outing with his Sunday school band. The kids went with their chaperone to the Vendome Theater.

"Louis stood up and started blowing," Jonah later reminisced. "Oh, he sounded so good. He sounded better than on records. I probably would have put down the horn, if it hadn't been for that. I didn't care nothing about anything but Louis."[2]

Jones went on to have an illustrious career in jazz, too, after learning from Pops's technique. He played with jazz violinist Stuff Smith's group, and then with Horace Henderson's band, in which he met another very great trumpet player, Roy Eldridge. Jonah joined Cab Calloway's nationally popular band in 1946.

Eventually Jonah recorded the song "St. James Infirmary" for Capitol Records. The stylish dancer Fred Astaire adored the record and wanted to dance to Jones's playing. Astaire went to the Embers, the posh Upper East Side club where Jones was playing, and invited him to work on a television show. That show won nine awards. "I got TV, records, and everything going because of that," Jonah recalled. It all began with the magic Pops had worked on Jonah.

In the late 1920s, Armstrong joined a group featuring the pianist Earl "Fatha" Hines in a band led by Carroll Dickerson. They went to work in the Sunset Café on Chicago's South Side. Louis played lead trumpet and was billed as the World's Greatest Trumpeter. The music was exciting. Then Armstrong was appointed bandleader, and Earl Hines became musical director. Louis and Earl were close friends. Armstrong could be somewhat forgetful, and Earl wrote the song "A Monday Date" as a reminder for Louis to keep a date. Reveling in the good times they had playing music together, they survived the rough life in Chicago, where gangsters ruled the clubs during those days of Prohibition and bootlegging.

Hines and Armstrong inspired each other to new heights of creativity, using each other's musical ideas freely. Hines had already fallen in love with the trumpet style of playing piano—playing long, fluid lines with his right hand in emulation of trumpet lines. During their days at the Sunset Café, a company called Okeh Records invited Louis to make recordings. In 1927 and 1928, Hines became a member of Armstrong's Hot Five and Hot Seven Bands—groups formed strictly to record in the studios for Okeh. Critics came to regard their recordings as among the best ever made by either Hines or Armstrong.

On one of those recordings, done in 1928, was Armstrong's extraordinary vocal and instrumental performance of a song called "West End Blues." The musingly scatted and hummed vocal version had a dreamy beauty. It sounded like a reverie. And it was a perfect jazz song because of his spontaneity and whimsical, carefree spirit. Some critics have called the recording the first genuine, thoroughly modern jazz song. The song fits the definition of jazz coined by a genius who came on the scene later—alto saxophonist Charlie Parker, who called jazz "a happiness blues."

Critic and musician Gunther Schuller thought "West End Blues" was the epitome of the jazz sensibility: "The first phrase startles us with the powerful thrust and punch of its first four notes. We are immediately aware of their terrific swing, despite the fact that these first four notes occur on the beat. . . . The way Louis attacks each note, the quality and duration of each pitch, the manner in which he releases the note, and the split-second silence before the next note . . . present in capsule form all the essential characteristics of jazz inflection."[3]

Few musicians have ever agreed upon an exact definition of jazz, but many say it must contain improvisation, and it must swing or imply dance rhythms derived from the old rhythmic device of syncopation. Syncopation is the rhythm achieved by stressing the weak beat in a measure of music. Louis Armstrong's style made him sound as if he wrote his swinging songs on the spur of the moment. His naturalness became a guide and a goal for every jazz singer and musician.

Pianist Ray Charles and singer Billie Holiday were two of the budding stars who fell under Armstrong's spell when they heard how he phrased and embellished songs. They loved the way he communicated feeling as a player and a singer. Trumpeter and singer Louis Prima would become well-known for singing in a scratchy voice like Louis's. Prima's trumpet style owed a great deal to Louis's, too.

Musicians revered Armstrong's style so much that they started calling him "Pops." (He acquired several nicknames. The most popular was "Satchelmouth" for his particularly wide, big mouth; a British critic shortened it to "Satchmo.") Gunther Schuller wrote that Armstrong's greatness lay in his light, open, airy elegance of tone, the easy swing of the beat, the subtle and varied repertory of vibratos and shakes, and a superior choice of notes and phrasing. Subsequent musicians have kept elaborating upon Armstrong's inventions. But it was Armstrong's original treatment of the chords and his tone, technique, and feeling that made musicians and audiences devoted to him.

Above all, Pops emphasized the melody, and "perhaps his greatest talent lay in his ability to transform even the most banal of popular melodies. To achieve this, he might anticipate one phrase, omit a weak or inferior one, substituting one of his own. He could take the most ordinary song and transmute it into a compelling instrumental experience."

Armstrong's solos were unique combinations of melodic variation and outright invention of melody.[4]

In 1929, Armstrong brought a whole band with him to New York and soon found himself out of work. The entertainment business was very unpredictable. But he landed a job for his band at Harlem's Connie's Inn. He was asked to sing and play a song called "Ain't Misbehavin' " by lyricist Andy Razaf and composer, pianist, and singer Fats Waller, a star in his own right. The song was the best one in an African-American show called *Hot Chocolates*, which opened downtown at Broadway's Hudson Theater on July 23, 1929.

Pops played in the show's band and then sang, unannounced, between the acts. The spotlight found him in the orchestra pit. He was a stocky, sparky fellow with a gravely voice. First he dazzled the audience with his trumpet playing; then he sang the song in his eccentric style. Critics wrote rave reviews about him. The word went out that Armstrong was the real hit of the show. A new star was born on Broadway.

He began writing books about his life and philosophy. He was a down-to-earth storyteller, in love with language. Though he had spent little time in school, he had an excellent instinct for choosing the right words to express his ideas. Among his insights: "All those years that trumpet comes before everything—even before my wife Lucille. Had to be that way. I mean, I love her because she understands that." (He eventually divorced Lil Hardin, married another woman who turned out to be a troublesome gold digger, divorced her, and then married his last wife, Lucille.) As a child, Louis had gone without shoes. When he became a millionaire, he said: "I don't try to get out of nothing. All I want to do is live good or bad, just live. If you're dead, it's all over. If I get poor, I'll still be happy. Like I always say, it's better to be 'once was' than 'never was.' "[5]

By 1932, he was so popular that he went to London, England, and played at the Palladium Theater with his big band. During a command performance for the king and queen, he called out to them from the stage, addressing them as "Kingsie" and "Queensie." They loved it. He was invited to dine with the royal family, and his earthy humor rose above all social class lines.

He continued to perform around the world for the rest of his life. In 1947, he played in a concert with a small group at Town Hall in New York. That was a turning point in his career. He broke up his big band and turned his attention to working with a small group, his All Stars, from then on.

In the All Stars at the start was his friend, trombonist and jazz singer Jack Teagarden, who was very influential on his instrument. Teagarden played the trombone with a spirit similar to Armstrong's. He used it for solos, freeing it from its usual role of playing a bass line accompaniment for the trumpet.

Also in the first All Stars performance were Rhode Island-born cornetist Bobby Hackett and a bright and fluid clarinetist, "Peanuts" Hucko, who was having a distinguished career in groups and recording studios. Hucko, who fit in snugly with the Dixieland and New Orleans-rooted swing-era musicians, would eventually join Armstrong's All Stars for a three-year stint beginning in 1958. He replaced a great early jazz clarinetist and Armstrong buddy named Barney Bigard. Barney had played his warm, distinctive style in Duke Ellington's band for years before joining the All Stars.

"It was one of the best parts of my life," reminisced Hucko. "That day I joined the band, I had to go to Corona, Queens [where Armstrong and his wife owned a house] to get on the bus. We were going to Old Orchard, Maine, to do a one-nighter. He was eating his red beans and rice. His wife Lucille told me to wait on the bus. Once we were moving, I waited about an hour, then got up my courage to talk to him. I said, 'Do you think we'll have time to run down a couple of things?' Armstrong answered, 'Don't worry, Pops. We all know our parts. You'll find yours.' "

A few days later, Hucko found himself playing at the Newport Jazz Festival in Rhode Island. Hucko knew the tunes, and he had rehearsed a little with the piano player, Billy Kyle. Trummy Young, the trombonist,

Jack Teagarden, a brilliant soloist on trombone, played with Armstrong's All Stars and led his own groups.

Louis Armstrong seeing himself in one of the countless thousands of backstage mirrors he encountered during his fifty years on the road.

Louis, and Peanuts harmonized for two bars sometimes, or eight bars at other times, on various tunes. "And I gradually got to learn what my part was," Hucko recalls.[6] It was about as regulated as the flight of a bird.

On tunes such as "After You've Gone," Hucko was hot and screaming along with Louis. For "St. Louis Blues," Hucko was swinging, fitting right in with the happy, group feeling. On "Tiger Rag," Hucko's dashing clarinet was joined and fortified by Louis's forceful trumpet. The only advice Armstrong ever gave Hucko was, "Play like you live"—play from the heart. The medleys in that concert and in all Armstrong's performances were all heart, with the joyful feeling of New Orleans music.

Armstrong had the physical stamina to travel for months on end in a bus that was too hot in summer and too cold in winter. He bumped along over rocky roads. He slept in his seat. Many musicians he hired came and went because they couldn't stand the hardships. But Armstrong never quit. His voice became raspier because of all the vibrant high Cs and upper-register straining that he had done with his horn. The raspier his singing voice became, the more popular he was.

He played in many movies. In time, he began to get better parts. His early roles had been silly and racially demeaning. In one role, he wore an animal skin. But his music always sounded wonderful, no matter what role he played. He had a small acting part that he handled with aplomb in *Paris Blues* with Paul Newman. Another fine trumpeter, Jack Butler, played in the same movie. Satchmo was a natural.

One of his best movies was *High Society,* with Grace Kelly, Bing Crosby, Frank Sinatra, and Celeste Holm. The movie opened with Armstrong traveling on a bus into Newport, Rhode Island, where he was going to play for a society wedding. He sang his great hit, "High Society," pronouncing the words "High—high—high—high—high—So - Ci - Uh - Teeeeeee." His music was sparkling and invigorating; without it, the movie would actually have been boring. He even made the bridal march swing at the end of the story and then launched into "High Society" again. The song made the movie end with the proper, upbeat, jubilant feeling.

Louis became a goodwill ambassador for the United States government despite his distress at prejudice against African-Americans and at the violence that erupted from the country's early attempts to desegregate schools and public facilities. He voiced his protests through the news media. J. Edgar Hoover, the powerful head of the Federal Bureau of Investigation, began to keep a file on Armstrong.

But Satchmo kept traveling for the government. His trumpet playing and his singing could reach across footlights, country borders, and political ideologies. He personally bridged the gap between the Western world's democratic societies and the dictatorships of Eastern Europe. Politicians and statesmen failed to reach understandings, but Satchmo kept the lines of communication between people open.

He was accused of selling out to commercialism because he sang and played so many popular songs, such as "Hello, Dolly" and "Mack the Knife." Of his singing, he said, "I sang some in Chicago, but it didn't get big until New York when the arrangers like Gordon Jenkins [in the 1950s] made up the arrangements with me singing that chorus. I just went along with whatever they brought for me. Everybody liked the singing and I never was trying to prove anything. Just wanted to give a good show."[7]

Actually, as he grew older, he couldn't play with shining perfection anymore, and he gave himself rest periods by singing. He was best known among jazz fans for singing and playing his standard, Southern-flavored jazz songs, such as "Muskrat Ramble," "I'll Be Glad When You're Dead, You Rascal, You," "Dinah," and "When It's Sleepy Time Down South." His fans had their favorite old Dixieland songs. He often introduced a song as "one of the good old good ones." He could give an audience goose pimples with his version of "St. James Infirmary," a song about saying farewell to his sweetheart, his "baby," lying cold and dead in a morgue. He ended with instructions about the fine clothes and jewelry he wanted to wear for his own burial. In Armstrong's version, the song mixed the sad and joyful feeling of the Second Line.

In his sixties, his heart began to fail. He kept going from hospital beds to his house in Corona, Queens, New York, to his bus on the road. Early in 1971, quite sick, he played at the elegant Waldorf-Astoria Hotel in

New York. Then he appeared as a guest on several television shows. In February, at his home in Corona, he recorded the narrative poem, "'Twas the Night Before Christmas," improvising his own jazzy slang expressions for some of the written words. The record is still played on radio stations during the Christmas season. He had a heart attack a few weeks later. Out of the hospital by May, feeling better—but bored—he decided to go back to work. All he wanted to do was continue his life as a real troubadour. He called the All Stars to come to a rehearsal in July. A few hours before they arrived, he died in his sleep.

Danny Barker convinced the City of New Orleans to erect a statue of Armstrong on the site of what had once been a slave market—the old Congo Square. Now it's a beautiful park with duck ponds. An entrance gate bears Armstrong's name. Barker gave a speech at the unveiling. He told people that serious students should listen to Armstrong's natural speech style and his immense humor and compare his style with the way popular music sounded before him. Before Armstrong, horn players had tried to sound like singers. Armstrong changed the emphasis. The goal of singers became to sound like horns with the fluidity, swing, and tone of Armstrong's style. Danny Barker reminded people at the unveiling how great Armstrong's contribution to American popular music and jazz had been.[8]

Even during the height of the popularity of the Beatles in the 1960s, Armstrong's "Hello, Dolly" went to the top of the charts. A NASA Voyager spacecraft sent into orbit in the 1970s carried a mixture of examples of American culture; it included twenty-seven different pieces of music, including one jazz tune, "Melancholy Blues," performed by Armstrong. In 1987, the movie *Good Morning, Vietnam* used Armstrong's recording, "What a Wonderful World," for the soundtrack. The whimsical, dreamy song, with Armstrong's scratchy but musing voice, became a major hit.

If it is possible to sum up the reasons for Armstrong's greatness and his enduring legacy, it lies in his conception of the role of the modern jazz soloist, as well as in his technique and his feeling, his taste and judgment, his joyousness and vitality as a player and innovator.

THREE

GREAT SWING-ERA HORN PLAYERS

PART ONE: THE TRUMPETERS

While Louis Armstrong was leading his Hot Five and Hot Seven groups on recordings, other record companies tried to find their own trumpet and cornet stars. Brunswick went after Jabbo Smith, and Victor recorded Henry "Red" Allen. Neither earned the fame and respect that Armstrong did, but both had their own worthy gifts. Roy Eldridge and Bix Beiderbecke also had successful careers as lead men.

JABBO SMITH

Jabbo, who was born in Georgia on December 24, 1908, was named Cladys by his mother, to complement a cousin named Gladys born around the same time. His mother was very poor and worked as a maid, so she took Cladys to the Jenkins Orphanage in Charleston, South Carolina, and visited him on weekends.

At Jenkins, Cladys began playing music and touring in the school band, which earned money to support the school. One of Cladys's schoolmates nicknamed the budding musician Jabbo as a play on words inspired by a cowboys-and-Indians movie they saw.

In the 1920s, Jabbo found first-rate jobs with touring bands and shows. He even made a recording of "Black and Tan Fantasy" with the Duke Ellington orchestra. By the late 1920s, he was working in Chicago, where Armstrong reigned as the trumpet star. But Jabbo attracted a great deal of attention for his vital and bluesy style as a player and singer. Some people thought he was as good as Armstrong.

Jabbo worked with Carroll Dickerson, Earl Hines, Erskine Tate, Charlie Elgar, Tiny Parham, and Fess Williams—all important bandleaders of their day—and he also led his own groups. But he liked to drink and spend too much time with girlfriends. By the 1940s, his career was in limbo. It wasn't until 1978 that he played before an appreciative public again, when he appeared at New York's Village Gate in a long-running popular show, *One Mo' Time*. Under the wing of his manager, Lorraine Gordon, wife of the owner of a famous jazz club, the Village Vanguard, Jabbo began working in New York and touring in Europe. His soulful, bluesy jazz singing won him a lot of praise. But bad health and old age prevented him from taking advantage of all his new opportunities. He died in a nursing home in New York's Greenwich Village in the 1990s.

HENRY "RED" ALLEN

Henry "Red" Allen was born in New Orleans on January 7, 1907. He played in his father's brass band, then went to St. Louis to join Joe "King" Oliver in 1927. He worked in the bands of Clarence Williams in New York and the Mississippi riverboat groups of Fate Marable, who brought many youngsters out of New Orleans. Armstrong, too, had played and learned to read music in Marable's band.

"Red" Allen sometimes sounded indistinguishable from Pops. Playing in several important bands of the period, Allen was admired as a leading trumpet soloist. In 1937, he played with a band that was being used to accompany Louis Armstrong. Armstrong's dominance prevailed; he was the star. Allen was, in a sense, demoted. He kept active by playing with New Orleans-rooted musicians, then joined a mainstream jazz movement at the same time that bebop, a more progressive style of jazz, began to revolutionize the jazz world. He made many recordings with such musicians as the great tenor saxophonist Coleman Hawkins, trombonist Kid Ory, and clarinetist Pee Wee Russell, among others.

ROY ELDRIDGE

More important than either Jabbo Smith or Red Allen, trumpeter Roy Eldridge learned his technique from Rex Stewart, who played in Roy's brother's band. Stewart was just a youngster himself then. He would go on to play cornet with distinction in Duke Ellington's band. Other trumpeters struck Roy as rough players with guttural sounds; he thought they were imitating Armstrong, and Eldridge felt more akin to the great early jazz saxophonists, Benny Carter and Coleman Hawkins. Roy preferred their smoother, cooler sound. But by the early 1930s, he came to admire Armstrong enormously and studied his recordings intensively.

Cited in the liner notes to *The Genius*, part of Armstrong's recorded legacy, Eldridge recalled the thrill of hearing Armstrong's original ideas: "He started out like a new book, building and building, chorus after chorus, and finally reaching a full climax. . . . The rhythm was rocking. . . . Everybody was standing up, including me. He was building the thing all the time instead of just playing in a straight line.

"I started to feel that if I could combine speed with melodic development while continuing to build, to tell a story, I could create something musical of my own," he said.[1]

Roy Eldridge was born on January 30, 1911, in Pittsburgh, Pennsylvania. By 1930, he was playing with Harlem-based bandleader Teddy

Hill, who broadcast from the Savoy Ballroom in Harlem. Roy thrilled many young musicians with his fast, intense trumpet style. He could play so many notes so fast that they sounded like vibrato, and he screamed on the high notes.

He left Hill to play in other cities for a few years, then went back to Hill's band in 1935, making recordings that attracted great notice. A young trumpeter, Dizzy Gillespie, growing up in Cheraw, South Carolina, heard the recordings and decided, "He's the man." Dizzy tried to copy Eldridge's playing exactly for a while.

Dizzy always said he was more influenced by Eldridge than by Armstrong. It's interesting to note that Eldridge, supporting his claim to be more influenced by Coleman Hawkins than "Pops" Armstrong, imitated on his trumpet a Hawkins solo on a recording called "The Stampede." And Hawkins himself said he was particularly influenced by Pops Armstrong. So in a roundabout way, Eldridge, and therefore Dizzy, fell under the spell of Pops's innovations.

Eldridge also played with Fletcher Henderson's band in 1935, then led his own band with his brother, Joe Eldridge, a saxophonist and arranger. Afterward, Roy formed his own ten-piece band and led it for three years at the Three Deuces in Chicago. He also had a radio show in town.

Armstrong had already begun to concentrate on pop music. Critics regarded Eldridge as the leading jazz trumpet soloist. White swing bands offered him jobs. He accepted one with Gene Krupa. As one of the first African-American brass section players in a white band, he recorded a highly praised version of the song "Rockin' Chair," probably his biggest hit. He had another nationwide success with his duet on "Let Me Off Uptown" with Krupa's band singer, Anita O'Day.

He would later tell a tale on himself about "Rockin' Chair." He had a record date with Gene Krupa, at which the other trumpeters were having trouble with sore lips. All the work fell to Roy. At the end of the session, Krupa called for "Rockin' Chair." Roy didn't feel like playing it; he was tired, and furthermore, he had been drinking. As he put it, "I had been tastin' to keep my spirits up." In fact, he had become "blind drunk."

He knew he shouldn't play another song, but Krupa insisted that he do it. The record became a big hit.

Coleman Hawkins told Eldridge about it, saying there was a wonderful tune out by "a bad trumpet player." (In the jazz world, "bad" means "good.") Hawkins and Roy put a nickel in a juke box and listened to the song. Pretty soon Roy recognized his sound. He was shocked and amazed.[2]

His next job was with another white big-band leader, Artie Shaw. The country was still strictly segregated. Eldridge suffered through many racial incidents that made his life hell on the road. Shaw tried to ease conditions for Eldridge, but, just as Shaw had failed to buck the system successfully on behalf of singer Billie Holiday a few years earlier, he couldn't prevail on behalf of Eldridge. Roy simply couldn't eat, sleep, or go anyplace with his white bandmates in comfort.

Once, he took the advice of Bon Bon, a popular African-American singer working with a white band. Bon Bon taught Roy to check into a segregated hotel by pretending he was the band boy renting a room for one of the musicians. The ploy succeeded for Roy. But then he picked up his own mail. After that, the hotel didn't enforce segregation anymore — at least not in his case.

Roy worked as a sideman on many of the best recordings of the 1940s, including "I Can't Believe That You're in Love with Me," with Benny Carter. By the late 1940s, Roy was working with a very successful concert series, Jazz at the Philharmonic, founded by a brilliant, courageous entrepreneur named Norman Granz. Granz never permitted his musicians to play before segregated audiences. It was astounding how well he succeeded in presenting the best jazz musicians under first-rate social and economic conditions in those days.

In 1950, to escape from competition with the progressive bebop players, Eldridge went to live in Paris. There he performed to great acclaim. Because he didn't have a work permit in France, he played only two sets a night at a popular club, Saint Germain de Près. He made a hit recording that he sang in French about French food items: sixty drinks, a little bottle of milk, a tomato, and mayonnaise were in the lyrics. Roy thoroughly enjoyed himself in Paris, where traditional jazz was honored.

He was a man with considerable charm, a big ego, and exceptional pride. He thrived on attention and praise, and he loved to play in jam sessions and compete with other players. Returning to the United States in 1951, he played in small groups with other leading jazz players, among them alto saxophonist, trumpeter, composer, and arranger Benny Carter; alto saxophonist Johnny Hodges, who had one of the most distinctive voices in Duke Ellington's band; and Roy's good friend, tenor saxophonist Coleman Hawkins. Eldridge, who was nicknamed "Little Jazz," and Hawkins, who was called "Hawk" and "Bean," recorded together for Verve Records in the 1960s. Roy also recorded with Ella Fitzgerald.

In 1970, Eldridge began leading a group at Ryan's, a popular midtown Manhattan jazz club that featured traditional pre-bebop music. In the group was Armstrong's former clarinetist, Joe Muranyi, who loved working with Roy. Despite all the racial problems Eldridge had faced earlier in his career, he never became embittered. He had never lost an iota of his self-respect and pride as a man and a musician. He looked everybody straight in the eye—African-American, white, or other—and treated them fairly and kindly, maintaining strict discipline at the same time.

Eldridge also played drums and piano. After he suffered a stroke in 1980, he kept his career going by playing piano and singing.[3] In the mid-1980s, his wife, who had been healthy, died suddenly. Nothing could comfort Roy. He stopped eating. Within a few weeks, he died, too.

BIX BEIDERBECKE

The most influential white jazz trumpeter of the era was Bix Beiderbecke. Born in Davenport, Iowa, on March 10, 1903, he probably never heard Armstrong, and Armstrong probably never heard Bix, either, until they developed their mature styles. Critics have usually described Louis as gregarious and extroverted, and Bix as subjective and sensitive. But they had a communion in their playing goals, innovations, and effect on listeners.

Roy Eldridge had his own exciting, fiery style in the swing era.

Admired by Armstrong, Bix Beiderbecke became the archetype of the "young man with a horn" in the Jazz Age.

Bix taught himself to play cornet—he never switched to the trumpet—by playing along with white Dixieland bands on records. The all-white Original Dixieland Jazz Band, a New Orleans group that was a big hit in 1917 in New York City, had recorded before the African-American groups from New Orleans.

Bix's parents didn't want him to become a jazz musician, and they sent him to Lake Forest Academy in Illinois—so close to Chicago that he was always sneaking away to hear jazz in the city. He was expelled from school and was soon leading his own band, the Wolverines, in Chicago. Bix went to hear Armstrong play on the South Side of Chicago. And the Wolverines' recordings in 1924 leave no doubt as to the impact of the influence of African-American jazz on gifted white musicians.

Bix moved on to New York City, where he joined a fine, early swing-era band led by Jean Goldkette. African-American musicians admired that band enormously. It went bankrupt because its lavish payroll for musicians outstripped its profits. Then Paul Whiteman hired some talented Goldketters. One of them was Bix. Another was saxophonist Frankie Trumbauer, Bix's close friend.

Operating on sheer genius, Bix didn't read music very well. Trumbauer tutored him and also tried to keep his young friend organized. Bix was a heavy drinker. He neglected every aspect of his health and daily life.

But his sound alerted and instructed every musician who heard him. The great white Dixieland players, who had imbibed the influence of New Orleans music—cornetist Jimmy McPartland, trumpeter Bobby Hackett, and the creative, rough-hewn, exciting clarinetist Pee Wee Russell, among others—paid homage to Bix by studying his solos. Cornetist Rex Stewart of Duke Ellington's band was mightily impressed by Bix. Another high compliment came from Pops Armstrong, who heard Bix and said they were striving for the same goal. Both were breathtaking soloists.

Bix died in 1931 from pneumonia, which was brought on by alcoholism. His music was a bright light gone too soon from the world, and his recordings in his pre-mainstream style are rarely played on the radio.

Among the best is "Singin' the Blues." In the 1990s, a collection of his recordings was released on compact disc. In his day, dubbed "The Jazz Age," he personified the romantic notion of the fast-living jazz man— "the young man with a horn."

PART TWO: THE SAXOPHONISTS

COLEMAN HAWKINS

Tenor saxophonist Coleman Hawkins, with his big, strong, earthy sound, became the most admired and influential player of the swing era. Every tenor saxophonist in every jazz generation has studied Hawkins's style and aspired to play with as much power and sensuality. He was the player who established the tenor saxophone as a force in jazz.

Hawkins was born in St. Joseph, Missouri, on November 21, 1904, into a musical family. His mother was a schoolteacher and organist. He began playing the tenor when he was nine and may have spent two years in college studying harmony and composition. He began working in Kansas City at the Twelfth Street Theater long before the area became famous as a jazz headquarters in the 1930s. He went on the road to California with Mamie Smith, a blues singer who had recorded an extremely popular song called "Crazy Blues" in 1921. By 1923, he was freelancing in Harlem, New York.

In 1924, Fletcher Henderson hired Hawkins, known as "Hawk," for a band going into the Club Alabam in New York. Hawk stayed with the band until 1934, establishing his own national reputation and enhancing the Henderson band. Then Hawk wanted to stretch out a bit and become independent. He may have contacted a popular British bandleader, or the bandleader may have called Hawk. In any case, Hawk's connection led to his first trip to England. He began by working with the British bandleader, went on to a group in Holland, then played in France and Switzerland.

In Paris, he made recordings with a legendary gypsy guitarist,

Django Reinhardt, and alto saxophonist Benny Carter. Carter, too, had found a warm welcome for his work in Europe. The Selmer Company, a famous manufacturer of wind instruments, hired Hawk to tour in England. He stayed so busy in Europe that he didn't get a chance to go back to the United States until 1939, near the start of World War II.

In New York, Hawk took a group into Kelly's Stable, one of many tiny jazz clubs on West 52nd Street. The street was a beehive of activity. The men in his band were thrilled to play with him; they regarded his group as a university. In October 1939, he recorded "Body and Soul," improvising exquisitely beautiful choruses that made the recording a commercial and artistic success. *Down Beat* magazine voted him the best tenor saxophonist in the world. His reputation was assured for the rest of his life.

By 1941, he was working with small groups in the Midwest, particularly in Chicago. Whenever he showed up in an audience to hear other musicians, they were flattered by his attention and struggled to perform with all the artistry they had. Then Hawk went back to lead his own groups in New York.

Actually, he was disappointed with the music in the United States. He had hoped to hear young musicians playing something refreshing and new, but for the most part the music scene hadn't changed in all the years he had worked in Europe. Only the young beboppers fascinated him with their experiments with harmonies. In February 1944, he led a group that included trumpeter Dizzy Gillespie and drummer Max Roach, two core members of the bebop revolutionary forces. The records made by this group were considered the first bebop recordings.

For another recording soon afterward, Hawk hired Thelonious Monk, the pianist called "the high priest of bebop." His compositions had unusual harmonies and spiky rhythms, and he played them with a quirky, flat-fingered style. Hawk was the only established musician to encourage Monk then.

By the late 1940s, Hawk began tacking back and forth between the United States and Europe. He played in all the major jazz festivals, sometimes co-leading groups with Roy Eldridge. Hawk toured with

Jazz at the Philharmonic and recorded for Prestige and Impulse. He appeared in one of the best jazz films, "The Sound of Jazz," produced by CBS as part of a series called *The Seven Lively Arts*. He made his only recording with Duke Ellington in 1962. For his frequent appearances at the Village Gate and Village Vanguard, two leading jazz clubs in New York, he led a quartet.

The young bebop players and their heirs tantalized him, but he never abandoned the style with which he had built his legend. In the late 1960s, his health began to deteriorate from drinking. He collapsed a few times on tours. He died in New York City in May 1969.

BENNY CARTER

Benny Carter became one of the most versatile, successful jazz musicians of his or any generation. Born in New York on August 8, 1907, he still performs in public, on alto saxophone and trumpet, with exceptional beauty in his tone. He could excite audiences in major concert halls in New York City. He could also lure people to jazz clubs in Greenwich Village, and he was chosen to lead a concert in Washington Square Park in the Village to kick off a festival in the mid-1980s.

By that time, he was playing frequently in public again after a career that had taken him to Europe and then Hollywood. Audiences might not have realized that when they listened to such haunting, romantic movie soundtrack songs as "Key Largo," they were listening to a composition by Benny Carter. Perhaps his most famous song is "When Lights Are Low."

Like most of the early players, Benny was self-taught. At sixteen, he was playing in professional bands, including Earl Hines's. He joined Fletcher Henderson's band in 1930 and became known for writing arrangements. By 1932, he was leading his own band with some of the foremost players of the early swing style—trumpeter Bill Coleman, trombonist Dicky Wells, tenor saxophonists Ben Webster and Chu Berry, pianist Teddy Wilson, and drummer Big Sid Catlett.

In 1934, Benny moved to England, where he had been invited to work as a staff arranger for the British Broadcasting Corporation. For four years, he advanced his career in England and Europe, at a time when few other Americans were welcome there. The musicians' union in England had wanted to keep out foreign competition. But he led international, interracial bands on the European continent.

Benny went back to New York in 1938, as the threat of a major war in Europe grew, and led his own bands. The first worked at the Savoy Ballroom in Harlem. Then he moved to Los Angeles. Some of his bands in the 1940s included the best young bebop players, such as drummer Max Roach, and the musicians they influenced, including trumpeter Miles Davis and trombonist J. J. Johnson. Benny hired Dizzy Gillespie in the 1940s when Dizzy had not yet made his own reputation as a bebop innovator. Benny liked Dizzy's ideas and wanted to give them a chance to be heard.

In the mid-1940s, Carter took bands on lengthy tours of theaters in the United States, traveling in the company of Nat "King" Cole. Carter was known not only as a first-rate musician and bandleader, but also as a calm, mild-looking man. He even had the courage to face down threatening mobsters in clubs.

His intellectual gifts and charm won him many friends. He never forgot a person's name and face. Increasingly in the 1940s, he composed and arranged for movies and television shows, and he established a long-lived, stellar career in the studios in California. At the time, the movie business was largely segregated. Benny Carter was one of the first African-Americans to cross the racial divide.

When jazz became more popular in public performances in the early 1980s, Carter led his own groups once more in festivals and clubs, on recordings, and for tours of Europe and Japan. His music has captured the modern flavor of each new decade—to a point. His tone retains the sweetness and warmth of the ideals of mid-century jazz. A lecturer at colleges, he has received many awards, including an honorary doctorate from Princeton University. With the physical agility and artistic ability of a much younger man, he led a highly praised concert at Lincoln Center in New York in the mid-1990s.

LESTER YOUNG

Lester Young also played on "The Sound of Jazz," the CBS television show that included Coleman Hawkins. It was Lester and singer Billie Holiday who attracted the most attention on the show. The communication between them was magical. In several ways, Lester eclipsed Coleman Hawkins in the 1940s, so great was Lester's direct influence on the playing styles of younger tenor saxophonists and musicians on other instruments. He had a slow, languid, soft-toned sound and a marked coolness to his style, in direct contrast to Hawk's big, earthy sound. Lester played poetic soliloquies. At the same time, his phrasing and rhythmic qualities presaged the revolutionary ideas of the beboppers.

Lester Young lived one of the saddest, most introverted lives of any jazz player. His friend Jon Hendricks, an important jazz singer and member of the vocal trio Lambert, Hendricks, and Ross, thought that Lester suffered so much because he was such a sensitive man. His sensitivity came through in his small-toned sound, which flowed like liquefied honey. For a long while he searched for mouthpiece reeds that would give him a bigger sound. But, as Billie Holiday tried to assure him, he didn't have to worry about having a big sound; his was perfect, and Billie confirmed that by nicknaming him "The Prez"—President of the Tenor Saxophone.

Born on August 27, 1909, in Mississippi, Young played with a family band led by his father. He broke away at the age of eighteen after an argument with his father. It may simply have been that Lester didn't want to tour in the Southwest with the band, preferring to go to Kansas. He had played many instruments by that time, including the alto saxophone. Some people thought his small tone originated from techniques he used during his early days on the alto.

He toured with a band based in Kansas, rejoined his family's band in New Mexico in 1929, then left again. By 1930, he was playing with a regional band called Walter Page's Blue Devils. One story says that the band went broke, and the musicians had their instruments confiscated;

48

Lester lost his alto. Without "loot" or an instrument, he said, he made his way to Kansas City, Missouri, in 1933.

Kansas City was becoming a jazz center. The corrupt political machine there, run by Tom Pendergast during Prohibition, made sure that night-clubs, which served liquor, catered to the high-rolling gamblers of the Midwest. The clubs hired jazz musicians as background entertainment.

In Kansas City, Lester acquired a tenor sax and clothes from William "Count" Basie's tenor saxophonist, Herschel Evans, and worked with many jazz musicians who would become famous. By 1934, Lester was friendly with Basie and played with his band in the Reno Club in Kansas City. He left to take Coleman Hawkins's place in Fletcher Henderson's band in New York. But Lester's sound was the exact opposite of Hawk's. The men in Fletcher's band had never heard such a laid-back, soft tone. They longed for Hawk's big sound and made fun of Lester, who left after a few months.

One lasting good came out of his few months with Henderson: Lester got the chance to jam in Harlem clubs and meet Billie Holiday. She was beginning to attract attention from jazz musicians and from Columbia Records. He nicknamed her "Lady Day," and Lady kept encouraging him.

Returning to Kansas City, Lester joined Count Basie's band again, and they recorded in 1936. Lester's solos on several tunes, "Lady Be Good" and "Shoe Shine Boy," charmed many musicians, particularly younger saxophonists. Dexter Gordon and Illinois Jacquet, rising stars in the 1940s, looked to him for inspiration. When Basie's band became famous and traveled around the world, Lester stopped in New York, where he and his Basie bandmate, trumpeter Buck Clayton, often record-ed with Billie Holiday for Columbia. The recordings became classics.

Lester chose to leave Basie in 1940. Don Byas, who would become well known for his work with the beboppers about to dominate the jazz scene, replaced Lester in Basie's band. Although Lester played remarkably well, his drinking was already affecting his decisions. He may have had a sloppy attitude toward band discipline. He may have refused to record with the band on a Friday the thirteenth, because of his superstitions. Or he may have given in to his sadness about the death of his pal, young Herschel Evans. Basie didn't tolerate Lester's odd habits well. But Lester's reputation remained illustrious during all the subsequent ups and downs in his life.

He took his own group into a 52nd Street club, then went to Los Angeles, where he worked with his younger brother, drummer Lee Young, who played with Nat Cole's group and Les Hite's band. Lee and Lester brought their group to Café Society in New York, the first racially integrated club in Greenwich Village.

In 1943, Lester joined Basie yet again. *Down Beat* named Prez the best tenor saxophonist in 1944. Tenor players listened to Lester for inspiration and instruction, among them Stan Getz, Zoot Sims, Lee Konitz, John Coltrane, and Sonny Rollins—all impressionable, gifted modernists destined for fame and fortune beginning in the 1950s and 1960s. Lester's unique tone, phrasing, melodic gifts, sweetness and bittersweetness, and long, flowing lines served as a bridge between the styles of older swing-era players and jazz modernists.

Not only did he credit the white saxophonists Frankie Trumbauer and secondarily Jimmy Dorsey, who led their own bands in the swing era, with influencing his style. Lester also loved the styles of singers Frank Sinatra and Dick Haymes.

In 1944, Lester was drafted into the army, taken completely away from music, and sent to a base in Alabama. There are several versions of his terrible experience in the army. One says he admitted to having smoked marijuana in his past. During the furor that erupted over that, he showed a photograph of his wife, who was white, to a white officer. That officer was so angry about Lester's interracial marriage that he engineered a court-martial and a five-year jail sentence for Lester on an invented drug charge.

Petrified, Lester was sent to the stockade at Camp Gordon, Georgia. He had the opportunity to brew some very potent alcohol in jail, and he was caught and given an extended sentence. Some versions of the story say that he was beaten up in jail. He began to lose his mind. Through the

Benny Carter, a great alto saxophonist, trumpeter, bandleader, arranger, and composer, has enjoyed a stellar career spanning more than six decades.

Tenor player Lester Young influenced modern saxophonists with his soft-toned, laid-back, liquid style and fresh approach to phrasing.

efforts of friends, Lester was released from jail, given a dishonorable discharge from the army, and returned to New York. In 1945, at his first post-military recording session, he played "These Foolish Things," considered one of his masterpieces.

Many say he was never quite the same man again. He toured with Norman Granz's Jazz at the Philharmonic. Some reports say he was confused by the bebop style surrounding him by then. Other people say his style became more emotionally charged. He always had an eccentric way of expressing himself, developing, in essence, his own language, both on his horn and in his speech. If he liked something, he had "eyes" for it. He called the woman who became his third wife his "pound cake." He drifted away from that marriage. In one recorded interview, which was aired on radio long after his death, he frequently swore.

Toward the end of his life, some friends went to see him in the midtown Manhattan hotel where he was staying. Lester was too weak to work. He may have earned as much as $50,000 a year during his Jazz at the Philharmonic tours. But in the late 1950s, he had no money left, and he drank uncontrollably. His friends, who were jazz musicians, cried after they left him. In March 1959, Lester died.

Among Prez's famous recordings as leader was "Jumpin' with Symphony Sid," which was used, with lyrics added to Lester's composition, as the theme song for Symphony Sid's well-known jazz disc jockey show in New York. Among his many great recordings, Lester played on "Doggin' Around," and his own songs "Tickle Toe" and "Lester Leaps In," Columbia recordings with Billie Holiday, and "Fine and Mellow" on the CBS production "The Sound of Jazz."

FOUR

MORE GREAT HORN PLAYERS OF THE FAMOUS BIG BANDS

Along came the Great Depression: The economy faltered, the stock market crashed, and banks closed. People lost their jobs, houses, and all their possessions, and they stood on bread lines for a bit of food to help them survive. Naturally people wanted an upbeat sound to help them forget their losses. So they grew tired of hearing even the most popular blues artists and their mournful songs. The big dance bands supplied the spiritual uplift that everyone craved during the 1930s.

Some bands had sweet sounds, and others became known for their swing. And all musicians wanted to get steady jobs with big bands in their heyday from the early 1930s to the late 1940s.

Horn players had a status similar to today's athletes. Not that musicians earned high salaries, but fans fell in love with their favorite players. Sometimes a single horn player gave a band its characteristic sound. As the bands toured the country to play at dances, people cheered for their idols. Hundreds of bands had very fine musicians, and some had great players whose styles were preserved forever on recordings. It would be impossible to write about all the great reed and brass players who thrived when jazz became the country's most popular music. But some of those players influenced generations of musicians to come.

DUKE ELLINGTON'S HORN PLAYERS

Duke built his band around his soloists. Among his horn players were trombonists Lawrence Brown, Joe "Tricky Sam" Nanton, Juan Tizol, who wrote the immensely popular songs "Perdido" and "Caravan," and eventually Quentin "Butter" Jackson. The most famous alto saxophonist and stylist of the swing era, Johnny Hodges, played for Duke. This was a time when the tenor players commanded the most attention, but everyone loved Hodges and his sultry, emotional sound.

Hodges, born in Cambridge, Massachusetts in 1907, flourished in Duke's band beginning in 1928. He occasionally left the band for short periods, quibbling with Duke about who was the greatest asset to the band, himself or Duke. But Hodges kept returning to play with the band until the end of his life in 1970. He could play an earthy blues, a sensitive, seductive ballad, or anything else Duke wrote for him. Above all, it was Hodges' expressiveness and tone that made his lines and melodies, no matter how simple he decided to keep them, turn to molten gold that flowed like a river.

Duke's band included clarinetists Barney Bigard and Jimmy Hamilton, both of whom also played tenor saxophone, and other great saxophonists of the era. Among them were baritone saxophonist Harry Carney, who gave the band tonal colors, and tenor saxophonist Ben Webster.

Alto saxophonist Russell Procope replaced Otto Hardwicke for one broadcast in 1946, when Hardwicke was visiting a girlfriend. Procope

54

Bandleader Duke Ellington had some of the most distinctive, adventurous horn players in jazz history, for whom he wrote compositions to show off their strengths. This 1937 photo shows trumpeters Rex Stewart, Cootie Williams, and Arthur Whetsol, trombonists Joe "Tricky Sam" Nanton, Juan Tizol, and Lawrence Brown, and reeds players Barney Bigard, Johnny Hodges, Otto Hardwicke, and Harry Carney.

ended up playing with Duke for the next several decades. And the mercurial, very gifted tenor saxophonist Paul Gonsalves went down in history for playing twenty-seven choruses on the song "Diminuendo and Crescendo in Blue" at the 1956 Newport Jazz Festival.

Trumpeters included Cootie Williams, who was famous for his "growls" on the instrument, and the astounding high note player Cat Anderson. Cootie replaced Duke's earliest cornetist, Bubber Miley. Others were cornetist Rex Stewart, trumpeter Harold "Shorty" Baker, and eventually throughout the 1950s trumpeter and fluegelhornist Clark Terry. By the 1990s, Clark was the only illustrious trumpeter from Duke's band still living and playing professionally—and receiving awards and honorary doctorates.

Clark, who was born on December 14, 1920, in St. Louis, Missouri, made a trumpet when he was a boy out of a piece of garden hose with a kerosene funnel for a bell. When he was about thirteen, he got his first real trumpet and played in kids' bands.

He sang in a Baptist church with his family, but he lived in a neighborhood filled with Sanctified churches. He imitated the exciting sound of the music in those churches—"Boooobcubaboonchibenboooonchili"—where the people were carried away by the fervor of their hymns. "We little kids used to sit on the curbs and listen. We liked the rhythms and the way they indulged in their services. Of course, we didn't go inside because we were Baptists."[1]

After high school and a stint in a navy band, Clark played with many groups. Among the best known of his early bosses was Lionel Hampton, who also employed tenor saxophonist Illinois Jacquet in the 1940s. Jacquet had a big hit with his solo on a tune called "Flying Home." For the rest of his life, he played it constantly for worshipful audiences who demanded it. Jacquet toured the world with his own band in the 1980s and 1990s. Its sound reminded people of the excitement of the swing era.

Launched by Duke Ellington's band, Clark Terry would go on to play for the bands of blues singer Eddie "Cleanhead" Vinson, Charlie Ventura, Count Basie, and Quincy Jones. In the 1960s, he joined the

NBC studio band for the *Tonight Show*, led by Skitch Henderson and Doc Severinsen; Clark stayed on until the show's star, Johnny Carson, moved from New York to Los Angeles. (A former Basie band trumpeter, Snooky Young, went with the Carson show, because he wanted a secure, regular paycheck for his family.)

Terry played in New York, led his own groups in famous clubs and all-star concerts, taught in colleges, and collected honors. The U.S. State Department chose him to lead goodwill tours to other countries. In all his experiences, he would always remember, "Louis Armstrong was my main inspiration. As I became more involved in music, Duke Ellington became my inspiration. We took it in from him by osmosis; all the good things about him, we absorbed."

The white bands led by Benny Goodman and Artie Shaw won the popularity polls in the United States in the swing era, while Duke's band, almost always made up only of African-Americans, registered as number one in England's leading jazz magazine of the swing era, the *Melody Maker*. (Throughout the decades, among the few white players in Duke's band were drummer Louis Bellson and Welsh-born baritone saxophonist Joe Temperley, whose smooth style and emotional appeal crossed all borders.)

Duke was destined for eventual recognition as one of the greatest composers of the twentieth century. And the men who played his music became—by association with him and because of his encouragement and support—among the best, most adventurous, and innovative jazz musicians in history. The horn players explored the capacities of their instruments. Trumpeters and trombonists used mutes in innovative ways to produce a greater variety of sounds, moods, timbres, colors, and dramatic phrases and soaring compositions than any other horn players in history.

COUNT BASIE'S HORN PLAYERS

Basie's blues-based bands had several incarnations. The first began in Kansas City in the 1930s. For a while in the late 1940s, when it had become too expensive for many to maintain big bands, Basie disbanded and led a small group. Then he formed a second great band in the 1950s. Both big bands had some very influential reed and brass players.

In the early band, players like trumpeter Buck Clayton, alto saxophonist and singer Earle Warren, soft-toned tenor saxophonist Lester Young, and Lester's exact opposite, the powerful tenorist Herschel Evans, gave the Basie band its strong, swinging, buoyant sound. Clayton was versatile; he could solo with strength and a commanding tone, and he could accompany and support the most delicate singers with sensitivity. Late in life, Buck led his own big band. He became especially noted for his arrangements. Lester Young and his melodic sound had a great influence on jazz history to come. Texas-born Herschel Evans played with a strong, outgoing, southwestern flavor.

When Basie took his band to New York's Apollo Theater in 1940, he brought with him other magnetic players who could rivet attention with their solos as well as their ensemble power—tenor saxophonist Buddy Tate, trombonists Vic Dickenson and Dicky Wells, and trumpeter Harry "Sweets" Edison. Sweets, whose nickname becomes self-evident to anyone who hears him play, mastered the art of playing with mutes. One of the stars along with Lester Young in the atmospheric, authentic, classic Count Basie band film *Jammin' the Blues*, Sweets went on to build a formidable, busy freelance career when Basie disbanded for a while.

Settling in Los Angeles, Sweets traveled with Jazz at the Philharmonic concerts, played in the studios, and recorded with Nat "King" Cole for the classic jazz album *After Midnight* in 1955. In the 1970s and 1980s, he led his own groups and played often with another Basie band alumnus, Eddie "Lockjaw" Davis. Later, Sweets co-led a band that recorded and toured with multi-reeds player and arranger Frank Wess in the 1980s and 1990s. Wess had played with Basie beginning in the 1950s.

In his late seventies, Sweets, who had been born on October 10, 1915, in Columbus, Georgia, could thrill audiences with understatement, even with just one note. He also had an exquisite imagination and tone for ballads. He toured in an acclaimed group of veteran players called Lionel Hampton and The Golden Men of Jazz, led by vibist Hamp, with

Count Basie's horn players, beginning with his band in the 1930s, have set unsurpassed standards forswing and dynamism. This 1940 shot of the band shows saxophonists Buddy Tate, Tab Smith, Jack Washington, and Lester Young, trumpeters Buck Clayton, Al Killian, and Harry "Sweets" Edison, and trombonists Vic Dickenson and Dickie Wells.

pianists Hank Jones and Junior Mance, drummer Grady Tate, bassist Milt Hinton, trumpeter Clark Terry, trombonist Al Grey, multi-reeds player James Moody, and tenor saxophonist Buddy Tate.

Other horn players matured in Basie's reorganized 1950s band. The band served as a springboard for their successful careers. Benny Powell, a courageous and virtuosic trombonist and group leader, had begun playing as a youngster in New Orleans. He was still playing, despite health problems, in the 1980s and 1990s. Trumpeter Thad Jones, a brilliant, modern arranger and composer, co-founded his own band with a drummer in New York in the 1960s. It played his distinctive compositions and arrangements. His work was used in colleges for arranging courses. Thad led Count Basie's band after Basie died in 1984. Frank Foster, also an eminent arranger and composer, took over leadership of the band after Thad's death about a year later. Then Grover Mitchell, a former Basie band trombonist, led the band beginning in 1995.

Basie's band nurtured so many fine arrangers that it was a virtual touring academy. Trumpeter Ernie Royal was another one. Ernie's brother, tenor saxophonist Marshall Royal, worked as the band's straw boss in the 1950s. That means he took charge of the band's day-to-day administration under Basie's leadership. Marshall even carried the money when the band traveled.

The rhythm section was always a rock solid quartet of men—Basie, the pianist, plus a bassist, guitarist, and drummer—but the horn players made the band a dynamo of swing. Basie always had some of the best horn players in jazz, such as trumpeters Emmett Berry, Joe Newman, Reunald Jones, Joe Wilder, Joe Keyes, Ed Lewis, and Waymon Reed. From the horns, the sound of courage became palpable. This was never a band for the faint of heart. Basie himself once told writer George T. Simon, "The band has always been built from the rhythm section to the tenors and then to the rest of the band." Simon commented in his book: "Interestingly, that's the way its most famous of all numbers, 'One O'Clock Jump,' is routined. It starts with just the rhythm section, then goes into a tenor-sax chorus, and eventually leads to the entire band."[2]

BENNY GOODMAN'S, ARTIE SHAW'S, AND WOODY HERMAN'S HORN PLAYERS

Benny Goodman himself was one of the greatest clarinet players ever. His tone and fluidity made him a masterful player of classical music and jazz. Among his few rivals was Artie Shaw, another extremely popular band-leader of the swing era. A third important bandleader, Woody Herman, also played clarinet. Although he didn't play with the same virtuosity as Goodman or Shaw, Herman had the perspicacity to hire great horn players.

Goodman, who was from Chicago, often went to hear Louis Armstrong play on the city's South Side. In 1935, Benny started his own band using Fletcher Henderson's arrangements. They were the best in the big-band world at that time, inspiring soloists with the power and rhythm of the ensemble backgrounds. Goodman's famed trumpet players were Ziggy Elman, Pee Wee Erwin, Bunny Berigan, and, most of all, Harry James.

Harry could play lead trumpet and swing a whole band, and he could also solo excitingly. He could read music with facility. He brought to the instrument a plaintive sound, not the bluesiness of the African-American culture. Some critics would say that James wasn't an authentic jazz trumpeter. Nevertheless, the Goodman band had a great trumpet section when James joined it.

The Goodman band played a famous concert that helped bring jazz and integrated jazz groups into the concert halls. The concert took place on January 16, 1938, at Carnegie Hall, and it included great visitors from other bands. Cootie Williams, Harry Carney, and Johnny Hodges came to represent Ellington's band. Count Basie arrived with Buck Clayton and Lester Young. Goodman's Ziggy Elman played such an exciting trumpet solo that it spurred the band to reach a new, exultant height. One critic saw men in white ties and tails dancing in the boxes. This was the concert that set the whole country to singing one of the band's most famous songs, "Sing Sing Sing."

In February 1939, Harry James began leading his own band, with which he would have great success. One of his first band singers was a virtual unknown, Frank Sinatra. James was a very nice guy, who encouraged young Frank, then sent him away with blessings when Frank got the opportunity to join a more popular band led by trombonist Tommy Dorsey.

With his own band, and his warm, sweet, and thrilling sound on trumpet, Harry James had many hit records. A charming, suave, dark-haired and handsome ladies' man, he went on to star in Hollywood movies and marry blonde actress and dancer Betty Grable. (Betty's legs were so beautiful that they were insured with Lloyd's of London for a million dollars.)

James's band had in its personnel for years a great alto saxophonist, Willie Smith, who had come out of Jimmy Lunceford's swing band. Smith was so highly regarded that he often played in both African-American and white bands. All the alto saxophonists listened to Smith for lessons in soloing and leading a section. Along with Benny Carter and Johnny Hodges, Smith was the starring altoist of the era.

Discovered while he was a student at Fisk University in Nashville, Smith graced the Lunceford band from 1929 to 1942. Lunceford missed Smith sorely when he left. For two years Smith played with bandleader Charlie Spivak, then joined Harry James for six years. He left to replace Johnny Hodges in 1951 and 1952 in Duke Ellington's band, and then went back to James until 1964. After that, Smith toured with Jazz at the Philharmonic and led his own groups. He died in 1967 in Los Angeles.

One of the reasons for the success of clarinetist Woody Herman's band, founded in 1937, was that he was so likeable. Musicians enjoyed playing for him, because he gave them plenty of support and encouragement. He ended in bankruptcy in the 1980s, after a lifetime of ups and downs. But he always paid his men well. He was also an exceptionally fine band singer, with a warm, expressive way of singing a romantic ballad. He was able to attract some of Duke's best horn players to record with his Herd, as his band was called. Trumpeters Carl (Bama) Warwick and Neal Hefti and popular tenor saxophonist Flip Phillips played in Herman's band.

Buddy DeFranco, who played in Tommy Dorsey's band in the 1940s, was one of the few clarinetists to make the transition from the swing era to bebop.

Clarinetist Woody Herman nurtured great players including the saxophone quartet the Four Brothers. This 1948 photo shows saxophonists Stan Getz, Al Cohn, Sam Marowitz, Zoot Sims, and Serge Chaloff.

Woody tried to retire in 1946, when the big bands were petering out. But a year later, he organized a second Herd, this one with saxophonists Stan Getz and Zoot Sims, who were both in love with melodies and very much under the influence of Lester Young, plus Herbie Stewart and baritone saxophonist Serge Chaloff; this exciting quartet was known as the Four Brothers. Others who passed through that group were Al Cohn and Gene Ammons. Saxophonist Jimmy Giuffre wrote arrangements for it.

The clarinet, the instrument of choice for many of the big-band leaders, no longer had cachet by the 1940s. Goodman, Shaw, and Herman enjoyed its heyday, and Armstrong would always use a clarinetist in his group, but modern jazz groups used one only as a doubler's instrument. That is, some who played tenor or alto or baritone saxophone as their main instrument might occasionally be asked to play clarinet (or flute) for a particular song. The high voice of the clarinet became a symbol of an earlier, less complicated era. In the modern jazz era to come, under the influence of John Coltrane, the soprano saxophone would emerge as a favorite second instrument for reed players.

Tommy Dorsey, the trombonist, set high standards for his bandmembers. Frank Sinatra later said he learned about phrasing for ballads from the way Tommy played his horn. Tommy first worked in bands led by Jean Goldkette and Paul Whiteman, then started a band with his brother Jimmy, a saxophonist. Tommy was difficult to get along with. He and Jimmy squabbled so much that they broke up and formed separate bands.

Called "the Sentimental Gentleman of Swing," Tommy created warm, romantic moods with wonderful rhythmic feeling for dancers. He hired many of the best musicians and arrangers, among them clarinetist Buddy DeFranco, one of the greatest modern players of the instrument, and trumpeter Charlie Shavers.

Stan Kenton was a latecomer to the big band scene as a leader in 1941. He presented jazz that was controversial because of its powerful screeching and blasting sound. Kenton's rhythms and harmonies were fascinating. Altogether, the band had a very modern sound, reflecting the growing tensions in the United States during World War II. Dixieland guitarist and club owner Eddie Condon, a well-known wit in the jazz world, congratulated Kenton on his accomplishment, after first saying, "Every Kenton record sounds to me as though Stan signed on three hundred men for the date and they were all on time."[3]

Kenton later hired more experienced, swinging musicians, among them tenor saxophonists Vido Muso and Bob Cooper and trombonist Kai Winding. A young baritone saxophonist, Gerry Mulligan, who would become a jazz world leader in the 1950s with his cool, pianoless group based in California, wrote arrangements for the Kenton band. In the 1950s, even Dizzy Gillespie and Charlie Parker toured with the Kenton band, when it was no longer economically possible for Dizzy to lead his own big bebop band.

This concise survey of great horn players of the big bands leaves out many wonderful, creative artists. In the big bands that toured the country, hundreds of exceptionally gifted young men with horns wove a spell for a dancing public seeking the sense of freedom that jazz has always provided.

CHAPTER FIVE

DIZZY GILLESPIE, CHARLIE "BIRD" PARKER, AND THE BEBOP REVOLUTION

Bandleader Cab Calloway had a wonderful reputation with musicians, because he paid them well and gave them a month's paid vacation for Christmas. In the band was an adventurous young trumpeter named Dizzy Gillespie. He had been a starving artist in Harlem, when a friend, Cuban trumpeter Mario Bauza, arranged for Dizzy to audition for Cab.

But Dizzy was also experimenting with harmonies by playing substitutions for the written notes. The band's bassist, Milt Hinton, recalled, "He was very deep into his chord changes and his substitutions which hadn't even hit this band yet, not at all. . . . Anybody making a substitution for a C chord? Nobody ever dreamed of that. If it was a C, you just played it, baby. And that was it."[1] Many people remembered Cab telling Dizzy, "Stop playing that Chinese music."

One day in 1940, Cab's band rolled into Kansas City for a theater date. When Dizzy stepped off the bus, an old friend greeted him and said, "Hey, man. There's a saxophonist you have got to hear. His name is Charlie Parker."

"Saxophonist? A saxophonist?" Dizzy said without much interest, with his soft southern drawl. "I've heard all the great saxophonists. There can't be nothing that I haven't heard among the saxophone players."

"Yes, you have to hear him," his friend answered.

Dizzy checked into a room at the Booker T. Washington Hotel, which was for African-Americans only. His friend brought Charles Parker Jr., nicknamed "Bird," a big man with a deep, quiet voice, into the room. Bird took out his alto sax and started playing. His phrasing fascinated Dizzy. "I can't believe the way he is playing," Dizzy later commented. "I've never heard anything like his style before."[2] Dizzy took out his trumpet and began to play, too.

"Bird played the blues like nobody else in the world. As fast as anybody else in the world. Keys didn't make no difference to him. I said, 'Here's the man.' I was completely convinced here was the Jesus of music. We played all day. We forgot to eat." That night, Dizzy recalled, "I barely got to the job with Cab."

Bird admired Dizzy, too, and would later tell an interviewer, "He was playing, as they say in the vernacular in the streets, a boocoo [beaucoup] of horn, just like all of the horns packed up in one." Bird's remarks, in one of his rare interviews, have been used many times in documentaries on Bird and Dizzy.

Dizzy would recall, "At first we stressed different things. I was more for chord variations, and he was more for melody, I think. But when we got together, each influenced the other."[3] He and Bird started to meet and experiment after hours in Minton's and Clark Monroe's

Uptown House in New York City; these were Harlem clubs where, in the early 1940s, the progressives jammed and developed a new style of jazz. In 1942, bandleader Earl "Fatha" Hines hired Dizzy and Bird.

Bird played with great naturalness. He didn't seem to have to plan where his creative instincts took him. He always knew all the right chord changes to play—the chord progressions—and how to play them. He had spent several years developing his style by intensive work. Dizzy honed his ideas through trial and error and careful analysis. He learned and adopted the flatted fifth chord, which gave bebop—the music he, Bird, and others were developing—its trademark plaintive sound.

Eventually, nearly everyone else would become intrigued with Bird's music—"the way he got from one note to the next," as Dizzy summed up Bird's heady style. Like Dizzy, Bird was iconoclastic. He took apart the principles upon which the swing era had thrived, and he made music that was more exotic, surprising, expressive, and unpredictable.

Dizzy, who was born into a large, poor family on October 21, 1917, in Cheraw, South Carolina, fell in love with music in grade school. As a teenager, he heard Roy Eldridge with Teddy Hill's band in a radio broadcast from Harlem's Savoy ballroom. Dizzy idolized and copied Roy's style. Instead of concentrating on developing a pretty tone, Dizzy focused on playing very complicated figures at fast tempos.

He got a scholarship to study at a segregated South Carolina agricultural college that had a band. Dizzy spent all his time analyzing music and playing piano and trumpet in the music room. When his widowed mother moved to Philadelphia, Dizzy dropped out of school and spent several years working with bands based in Philadelphia. He began to teach himself how to arrange music.

Working with Lucky Millinder's band in Harlem before joining Hines's band, Dizzy made a recording of "Little John Special." On that tune he played a three-note phrase—a lick or riff, as jazz musicians call it—with a big interval leap from a low register to a high one and back down to a low one. The phrase was plaintive, intense, and jubilant all at once. It became the basis for one of his best-known compositions, "Salt Peanuts."

"Salt Peanuts" soon became very popular with progressive musicians. Everybody played it. Decades later, musicians still added the appealing, off-kilter three-note riff to other songs. Dizzy wrote many of his greatest songs in the early 1940s. First came "A Night in Tunisia," then "Salt Peanuts," which he would write with Bird. Dizzy's arrangements for compositions by jazz pianist Thelonious Monk and Broadway songwriter Jerome Kern became parts of the songs, too.

Dizzy spent hours working with Monk, who was playing at Minton's Playhouse in the early 1940s. Monk taught Dizzy invaluable lessons about harmonies. Dizzy would recall, "I could always find chords on the piano, and people helped me. . . . I'll never forget the day that Monk showed me a . . . chord . . . that opened up new avenues. I had never heard of that chord before. . . . I used it on [the arrangement of Monk's tune] 'Round Midnight,' and on many others, on 'Woody 'n' You,' [which Dizzy wrote for Woody Herman] I used that particular chord. . . . Every time I'd write something, that chord would be there someplace for the resolving."

Like Dizzy, Charlie "Bird" Parker came from a background with little obvious promise. Born on August 29, 1920, in Kansas City, Kansas, Charlie soon moved with his mother to Kansas City, Missouri, a hotbed of jazz activity. A Texas-born alto saxophonist, Buster Smith, lived there for a while. Young Charlie, just beginning to play alto, would stand outside a house where Buster played in jam sessions.

People laughed at Bird's early efforts. But he went to "woodshed" (practice) in the Ozarks. There, he learned from older players, practiced constantly, and listened to his heart for directions about what route to take, what note to play, and how to phrase his melody lines and embellishments. Then he went back to Kansas City and played in Buster's band.

Bird was on the road in Kansas with a group of musicians, heading to a gig, when their car hit a chicken. He insisted on taking it to a woman who owned a boarding house where the band was staying. The musicians nicknamed him "Yardbird," which eventually became just "Bird."

At age sixteen, Bird married his girlfriend, and they lived in his mother's boarding house. Then Bird was in an auto accident with musicians on the way to a job and suffered a broken spine and ribs. Doctors gave him morphine to ease his pain. One legend says that when he got out of the hospital, he kept looking for pain-killing drugs. He may also have come to crave a "high" feeling. Another legend says that a Kansas City hipster taught Bird to use drugs.

By age seventeen, he was playing with bandleader Jay McShann. McShann, a fine blues-rooted pianist, tolerated Bird's heroin habit and strange behavior because Bird could play so well. But Bird fell asleep on the bandstand. He didn't show up on time for jobs. He often pawned his horn to get money for drugs. He was the most aggravating budding genius one could imagine.

Bird felt the urge to go to New York, the center of jazz activity, so he asked his wife for a divorce and suggested she and their son stay with his mother. Bird told his wife he thought he could become a very great musician, if she would let him go free. She agreed to the divorce.

Working as a dishwasher in one club where the great pianist Art Tatum played, Bird went to jam late at night at Clark Monroe's Uptown House. According to a jazz legend, Bird gave birth to bebop by jamming at Monroe's. The tale is too simple, because many people were paving the way for bebop's development. Among others, Dizzy and Monk were playing unusual harmonies.

But one night, while playing a solo above the chords of "Cherokee," a popular tune, Bird went farther from the written melody than any jazz player had ever done before. He used the higher notes of a chord—ninths and thirteenths—as a melody line and backed them with appropriately related chords. His improvisation transformed "Cherokee" into a separate tune that became known as "Ko Ko." Bird realized he could create a new repertoire based upon the chords of older songs. Within a few years, when the beboppers got their chances to record, he would record his classic version of "Ko Ko" and many other new songs. His gifts as a brilliant improviser caught the attention of the critics.

Earl Hines paid off Bird's debts to Jay McShann, bought Bird a tenor saxophone, and took his band all over the country to play for dances, which usually paid well. The young musicians in his band weren't stars yet, but their fire appealed to him and to audiences. The band never recorded, because the musicians' union called a strike against recording companies to get better working conditions. But people who heard the band in person thought it was exciting.

Also in the band was Sarah Vaughan, who would become one of the most important jazz singers in history. She revered the way Bird played. Dizzy noticed, "She didn't want to know about nothing but Bird's music."[4] Dizzy wrote arrangements for Sarah while in the Hines band. One was for the song "East of the Sun, West of the Moon," but it was minor in feeling and slow for dancing—too different for Earl to want to feature with his band. Dizzy was in love with his experiments and wanted to have more opportunity to show off his own tunes, such as "A Night in Tunisia." This would become his most famous composition.

Dizzy later told how he had been sitting at a piano one day: "And after hitting this chord, a D minor, I said to myself, 'Boy, that's a nice chord change.' And the melodic line of 'A Night in Tunisia' was in the chord. . . . I had to write a bridge for it, of course, and I didn't have a name for it." The D minor chord had come to Dizzy from Monk during a jam session at Minton's in Harlem. Then Dizzy wrote a bridge—a middle for the tune—and added a Latin rhythm.

Billy Eckstine, a popular baritone singer with Earl Hines in the early 1940s, left Hines's band by 1944 and started his own band, for which he hired Dizzy as musical director. Then Billy went looking for Bird, who was playing at the Rhumboogie, a club on Chicago's South Side.

For Billy's band, Dizzy wrote an arrangement for a tune called "Good Jelly Blues," a sequel to Billy Eckstine's big blues hit, "Jelly, Jelly," done with the Hines band. One day, the band's arranger, Walter Gil Fuller, went to a big-band performance at the Brooklyn Armory in New York. On one side, Jimmy Lunceford's swing band was playing, and on the other side, Billy Eckstine's was holding forth. The crowd went from one bandstand to another for a while. Then everybody settled in front of Eckstine. "So that's the first time that I got the inkling that the real change had taken place. . . . That was the first night that we knew," Gil recalled about the changing of the guard in the jazz world.[5]

Some audiences and critics still resisted bebop's odd sounds and said they were wrong notes. Actually, to play bebop, musicians needed a well-defined rhythmic sense, a knowledge of harmony, and very sharp abilities on their instruments.

The clique of experimenters often met at Dizzy's tiny apartment in Harlem, where Dizzy's wife Lorraine cooked for them. About Parker, she said, "Bird was a quiet, gentlemanly man. The only thing wrong with him was that [heroin] habit."[6] Though she felt sorry for him, she noticed that no matter what Dizzy did to help Bird stop taking heroin, Bird couldn't quit.

Dizzy told people he wished he could take Bird into his apartment and force him to get well. But Dizzy was struggling to make a living and establish a career. He didn't have the time or money to spend nursing Bird. And Bird was stubborn and didn't walk away from his habit.

Dizzy loved to give music lessons to young players, teaching them harmonies and rhythms. Bird also taught youngsters, but primarily by example. Whenever he walked into clubs, other musicians became so flustered by his presence that they could hardly keep playing. Dizzy was a mischievous man with a zany sense of humor. When Eckstine was

Bandleader Dizzy Gillespie, the great showman, trumpeter, composer, and bebop revolutionary, had his early successes on 52nd Street.

singing, Dizzy made pantomime gestures to the audience, communicating that Eckstine had false teeth. That type of behavior had earned Dizzy his nickname years earlier. He had charisma, and he loved to be the center of attention.

Dizzy decided to try leading a band himself. Eventually he won the New Star Award from *Esquire* magazine's jazz poll. He co-led a band with a strong bassist, Oscar Pettiford, an *Esquire* Gold Star winner, at the Onyx Club on 52nd Street. Dizzy found himself in the company of singer Billie Holiday, another Gold Star. Dizzy's morale got a big boost from the company he was keeping. He sent a telegram to Bird to come to the gig. But Bird had gone to Kansas City and never got the message.

Tenor saxophonist Don Byas, who had already played with Count Basie and other bands, began working with Dizzy's group, making it a quintet. Byas wasn't a bebop player, but he was one of the best saxophonists of his day—when he wasn't drunk. When Byas drank, Dizzy argued with him right on the bandstand. Dizzy couldn't tolerate unprofessional behavior. He had too much at stake—the music, his ambition, his ideals.

For Dizzy, the days on 52nd Street were a rough-and-ready time. One night he got into a life-threatening knife fight with some white sailors who objected to his talking to a very light-skinned singer. Before anyone got hurt, the Shore Patrol arrived and arrested the sailors.

Aside from his gigs, Dizzy wrote arrangements for such big name leaders as Jimmy Dorsey, Woody Herman, and Boyd Raeburn. Young musicians in all the bands wanted to play some of the new music. Dizzy put his bebop phrases into an arrangement for Dorsey called "Grand Central Getaway." Dizzy also introduced something new—the double-up arrangement, in which the rhythm section played in one tempo while the horn section played twice as fast. Dizzy never said his writing was superior to everyone else's. But he knew he was writing music with a fresh sound, different notes, and new phrasing. "In the music of the forties, our creativity was at our highest point, with Bird and Monk," he later commented. "They represented the age of World War II."

Dizzy wrote arrangements and played for a band that Coleman Hawkins led in 1944, and their recordings together became known as the first bebop recordings. A rising young critic, Leonard Feather, took an interest in the beboppers. He convinced Guild, a small company, to record Dizzy and Bird. The quintet also played at the Three Deuces on 52nd Street.

The bebop recordings made by Dizzy and Bird in February and May of 1945 included such songs as "Groovin' High," "Dizzy Atmosphere," "All the Things You Are," "Shaw Nuff," "Lover Man," "Salt Peanuts," and "Hot House." They circulated throughout the country and spread the word of the style's arrival and importance. Young musicians listened and learned the style by ear. One of the great bebop songs of the time, based on the chord changes of "How High the Moon" and renamed "Ornithology," became a particularly popular bebop tune. All young musicians learned to play it.

In November 1945, Charlie Parker led a sextet at another landmark recording session, with Dizzy playing trumpet and piano. Young Miles Davis played the trumpet when Dizzy played piano. The group played pure bebop songs and arrangements.

Billy Eckstine's manager helped Dizzy form a big band, which Bird joined. Dizzy took it on tour in the South. But the people wanted to dance and hear the blues. They hated Dizzy's band. Dizzy went back to New York to try to recover his losses.

On 52nd Street, though, the audience appreciated bebop. Dizzy was thrilled by the way he and Bird communicated on the bandstand. "Shaw Nuff," a song they wrote for their manager, Billy Shaw, and which they recorded for the little Guild label with Dizzy's quintet, eventually became a demonstration record at the Juilliard School of Music in New York for lessons in ensemble playing.

On WKCR, Columbia University's radio station, Dizzy marked the fiftieth anniversary of his recording debut. He reminisced about his best times with Bird: "Yard and I were so close, so wrapped up in one another, that he would think 'three,' and I would say 'four,' and I would say 'seven,' and he'd say 'eight'. . . . It wasn't difficult for us, really together, sometimes it sounded like one horn playing, and sometimes it was one horn, but sometimes it was both of us sounding like one horn."

Miles Davis, starting his career in the 1940s, marveled at the synchronization between Bird and Dizzy and at how fast Bird could play. Miles was slowly developing into a player in the middle register of his instrument, and with the most beautiful and haunting tone in the history of jazz trumpet. His day would come in the 1950s and 1960s, when he became the country's most influential jazz player.

But in the 1940s, Dizzy and Bird were the heroes. They faced just one insurmountable problem: Bird fell asleep on bandstands, nodding off from heroin use. They never fought openly about it. But Dizzy, along with Max Roach, begged Bird to stop throwing his life away. Bird said he was getting famous through music for one reason: to call attention to the evils of drug addiction. He had been put on earth to scare people away from drugs. Max knew that Bird would say anything to justify his helplessness against the force of his habit.[7]

Dizzy received an invitation to take a quintet to Billy Berg's club in Los Angeles. Berg had owned clubs since the 1930s, and he had even ended racial segregation in the audiences in the 1940s. Artistically and commercially, Berg was taking a chance by booking the beboppers for a Los Angeles audience, which liked swing-era musicians and singers. So Berg booked Dizzy and his quintet, including Bird, as the intermission entertainment.

Dizzy hired a sixth person, vibist Milt Jackson, to go to California, because Dizzy was afraid that Bird wouldn't show up for all the performances. Dizzy was right to worry. Bird missed performances. Furthermore, Californians didn't like the new music. Berg asked Dizzy to sing a little, and he did it reluctantly. He also socialized with other musicians and jammed and recorded with them on the West Coast. That cheered him up. He was very happy when the gig at Billy Berg's ended.

Bird "was out in the jungle somewhere, just lost, man," said the drummer Stan Levey, whom Dizzy had taken to California with the group.[8] Dizzy left Bird's money and airline ticket back to New York at Bird's hotel. That was the last time they saw each other for more than a year.

Bird continued working on the West Coast, even though he was very sick. In his last recording session for Dial Records in 1946, he played a version of "Lover Man" that came to be regarded as a classic. But Bird became so sick from drugs, alcohol, and mental confusion in California that he was taken to a state hospital called Camarillo, where he was truly cured of his drug habit—for a while.

After he got out, he stayed on the West Coast to work. One day, while riding in a taxi, he composed a song called "Relaxin' at Camarillo." Other musicians struggled to play it so they could learn from Bird's improvisatory genius.

Back in New York, Dizzy found himself in demand in two clubs on 52nd Street. He hired alto saxophonist Sonny Stitt, who had patterned himself after Bird. By now, because of Bird's excellence, everyone wanted to play alto sax instead of the tenor. (And Stitt, like many other musicians who worshipped Bird, used heroin. Musicians hoped that drugs would help them play as well as Bird did. Bird warned them against drugs, but they didn't listen. Some musicians died of their habits. Others eventually quit and straightened their lives out. For a while, heroin plagued the jazz world.)

Dizzy took a small group including Stitt into the Three Deuces club and a big band into the Spotlight club. Billy Eckstine, who was breaking up his band, gave his uniforms, music, and everything else to Dizzy. With Walter Gil Fuller, Dizzy prepared the arrangements for the big band opening at the Spotlight. They used music by Thelonious Monk and John Lewis, a classically trained pianist just home from the army. John Lewis also played with the group.

Alto saxophonist Charlie Parker was the stylistic genius of the beboppers' approach to music and influenced every player on every instrument from the 1940s to the present.

And Dizzy hired a talented young tenor saxophonist, James Moody, who was partially deaf. Moody overcame his handicap, playing many of the reed instruments with virtuosity. He became intensely devoted to Dizzy. For the next four years, Moody toured with Dizzy's band wherever it could find engagements. Moody, taking a vacation in Paris to recover from the strain of the road, improvised a song called "Moody's Mood for Love" from the changes of "I'm In The Mood For Love." His tune became one of the most popular jazz compositions ever.

Bird returned to New York in 1947 and joined Dizzy's band. He looked very well, but soon he was hooked on drugs again. At one performance, he showed up late and fell asleep on the bandstand. Dizzy became so upset that he asked Gil Fuller, his tough musical director, to fire Bird; Dizzy couldn't do it himself.

After that, Bird led his own groups and Dizzy led his; they didn't often play together anymore. Dizzy's band was going strong in 1947 when he asked his old friend, the Cuban musician Mario Bauza, to recommend a conga player. Mario found a very exciting conguero, Chano Pozo, newly arrived from Cuba. They had great success with a song called "Manteca," a collaborative effort between Dizzy, Chano, and Gil. "Cubana Be Cubano Bop," written by experimental American jazz composer and bandleader George Russell, was another success for them.

Dizzy appeared at Carnegie Hall with Chano Pozo, who unleashed his primitive power to spur the band on. The concert was a great success. Bird came onstage to hand Dizzy a rose and kissed him. Dizzy thought Bird had spent his last penny for the flower.

Despite his problems with heroin, Bird enjoyed a period of great creativity in the late 1940s and early 1950s. His recordings for the Dial and Savoy companies in 1947 and 1948 are among his best. He led quartets and quintets including Miles Davis, Max Roach, pianist Duke Jordan (and sometimes Bud Powell or John Lewis), and bassist Tommy Potter. He performed on 52nd Street and traveled to Europe, where he made many recordings. Based on the blues and the popular songs "I Got

Rhythm," "Honeysuckle Rose," "Lover, Come Back to Me," "Embrace-able You," and "The Way You Look Tonight," to name a few, he impro-vised classic bebop songs.

By 1948, Bird was the most influential bebop musician. He moved on to the Mercury label and recorded Afro-Cuban jazz for Norman Granz. He also made controversial recordings with string instruments. Some people loved Bird's romantic sounding music with strings. Other peo-ple—call them bebop purists—favored Bird's intense sound dominating small groups. Other jazz musicians would subsequently record with strings to great effect.

As writer Len Lyons described Bird's sound in small groups: "The virtues of 'Ko Ko' are what make all of Parker's work compelling. His tone on alto sax is a cutting, searing one that penetrates to the listener's core. Like it or not, Bird commands attention, communicating with inner urgency. The swing, fury, and agility of his technique are too obvious for comment. His phrasing, splintered into jigsaw-like patterns, fits togeth-er miraculously as an integrated whole by the end of the piece. . . . The music's overall hotness—comparable to Armstrong's trumpet style—is due to Parker's delivery: his lines can be likened to a shower of sparks."[9]

Dizzy also took his band to Europe, where the financial arrangements were messed up by a crooked Swedish promoter. But at the last stop, in Paris, the band's shows were sold out. Bebop took Paris by storm in 1948.

For a while in the 1950s, Dizzy's fortunes took a nosedive. Fashions in popular music and jazz changed. Bebop, with its aggressive sound and fast tempos, sounded outdated, or too strident in its pure form. Pop artists were profiting as bop became commercialized. A cooler, more laid-back style of jazz was becoming trendy. Dizzy had to break up the big band and work with a small group. Sometimes he even took gigs in small clubs in Queens and toured with Stan Kenton's band. It took him a while to get to play with his own group at Birdland, the leading jazz club of the era.

Bird also fell on hard times. In 1951, his cabaret license, which allowed him to play in New York clubs, was taken away by the police, because of his drug addiction. He didn't get the card back until about 1953. For a while even after he had it again, Birdland, the club that had been named for him, didn't let him perform there.

Despite such challenges, Bird and Dizzy influenced everyone on all the instruments. Fats Navarro, who died young, had a better tone on trumpet than Dizzy, and he stressed beautiful melodies. Howard McGhee was a wonderful trumpeter who started in the bebop era. Trumpeters Miles Davis, Red Rodney, and Clifford Brown, tenor saxophonist Dexter Gordon, altoists Jackie McLean, Charles McPherson, Julian "Cannonball" Adderley, and Charlie Mariano, to name only a handful, carried on the work of the founding beboppers.

Bird was inspired not only by the blues and Armstrong's music and the chords of pop and standard songs, but by European classical music from Ludwig van Beethoven to Igor Stravinsky to Claude Debussy and the French Impressionists. He imbibed the world's culture as gluttonously as he did drugs and alcohol. His rhythms, phrasing, and melodies still fascinate critics. Every morning on WKCR in New York City, jazz historian Phil Schaap hosts "Bird Flight," a program of Parker's recordings.

In 1953, Bird and Dizzy played together in a concert billed as the "Greatest Jazz Concert Ever," at Massey Hall in Toronto. The group included pianist Bud Powell, drummer Max Roach, and bassist Charles Mingus. Dizzy knew that Bird was having a very hard time finding work. He was so unreliable that few people hired him. He looked very bad—puffy, overweight, simply very sick—a far cry from the young man whose music had lit a path for countless musicians.

One night, Dizzy went to a nightclub during a break in his own gig at Birdland to hear trumpeter Charlie Shavers. He saw Bird in the audience.

Bird said to Dizzy, "Save me."

Dizzy asked what he should do. Bird said he didn't know, but just "save me."[10]

Dizzy didn't want to take Bird into his group, because he feared Bird wouldn't show up for work. That was Bird's usual routine. Bird played at Birdland in March 1955. Then, on his way to an out-of-town gig, he went to visit a patroness of jazz, a European-born baroness and heiress who lived in a luxury hotel. He became ill there, and the baroness called a doctor. Bird refused to go to a hospital and spent several days in bed at the hotel. He had married three women, left them all, and even left his mistress with whom he had had two children. By that time, the baroness was Bird's only refuge and protector. Watching television with her, he collapsed and died on the couch. He was thirty-four years old.

At the time of his death, his reputation had not spread very far outside of jazz circles. His addiction had prevented him from putting all his energies into spreading the gospel of his own genius. That work would be left to others.

Dizzy went down to the cellar of his house and cried for a week after Bird died. His wife worried about how upset he was. Dizzy had also not yet recovered from the dip in the commercial fortunes of bebop. He was working at any job he could find.

With his natural persistence, and advice and encouragement from his wife and friends, Dizzy would secure his place in the sun. He was going out the door one day to play for Jazz at the Philharmonic when he got a call from the State Department asking him to lead a big band on a tour of the Near East. It turned out to be wildly successful and led to another goodwill tour, again led by Dizzy, in South America.

Dizzy lived a long time, spending most of his life on the road, playing classic bebop and adopting to changing times for adoring audiences. He always promoted the compositions and contribution of Bird, heralded the influence of Afro-Cuban and Latin music, which he loved, and encouraged young musicians. He won many awards, including a Kennedy Center honor, and at least a dozen honorary doctorates.

In the last years of his life, in the 1980s, Dizzy was the leading superstar in jazz—a chief among chiefs. As one trumpeter said to another in the audience at a Gillespie concert, "We've come to hear our king."

Dizzy noticed how succeeding generations of adventurous younger musicians had taken jazz in new directions. New generations always want to do something revolutionary. And Dizzy realized that all of their new ideas were spawned by bebop. He wanted to be remembered as a "major messenger," he said. It would become clear to everyone that he succeeded. And Bird had been the power behind the throne.

THE JAZZ HORN TREE

This tree focuses on the innovators and some pivotal jazz horn players, particularly the trumpeters and alto and tenor saxophonists. Many important virtuosic players have been omitted from this tree, although they are included in the book; any attempt to include everyone would make the tree confusing and unwieldy, because of the sheer numbers of players on various instruments who have had an influence.

EARLY 1900S

Buddy Bolden was among the first important cornetists. Next came *Bunk Johnson*.

Sidney Bechet

Freddie Keppard had his own band, and *Joe "King" Oliver* played cornet in trombonist *Kid Ory's* popular band. Soprano saxophonist *Sidney Bechet* was one of the most important horn players in New Orleans. Bechet's student and friend, clarinetist *Jimmie Noone*, also became a notable player. Another fine clarinetist who grew up in New Orleans was *Barney Bigard*. Joe Oliver went to Chicago, leaving his place in Ory's band to a younger cornetist, Louis Armstrong.

BETWEEN 1910 AND 1922

Louis Armstrong, born August 4, 1901, developed into a great cornet player in New Orleans.

In Texas, *Jack Teagarden* began playing trombone in about 1915. He would become one of the most important early jazz trombonists, influenced by his southwestern birthplace and the innovations of the New Orleans players, particularly Armstrong.

FROM 1922

Armstrong joined Joe "King" Oliver's Creole Jazz Band at the Lincoln Gardens in Chicago. Switching completely to trumpet, Armstrong came to be regarded as the most influential and innovative jazz player. By embellishing everything— "blowing on the changes," as jazz musicians called the technique of playing all the notes in the chords as well as notes that the chords suggested—and by making his blend swing with a characteristic two-beat New Orleans rhythm, he created the foundation of modern jazz. He bent the notes, too, gliding from one note to another for a more emotionally stirring sound. And he played legato with long lines, instead of staccato, as trumpeters and cornetists before him did.

Noone and Teagarden also migrated north and established their careers. Teagarden's style meshed so well with Armstrong's that eventually he played in Armstrong's group, the All Stars, beginning in 1947. Both Armstrong and Teagarden sang in styles that emulated their horn playing.

FROM 1927

Duke Ellington led a jazz band and took it to the glamorous Cotton Club in Harlem, New York. He wrote striking, original compositions, tailoring them to the strengths of his musicians, such as trumpeter *Cootie Williams*, clarinetist *Barney Bigard*, and alto saxophonist *Johnny Hodges*. His band toured Europe in the 1930s. The personnel would change throughout the decades until Duke's death in 1974, but it always included some of the best horn players in jazz history. They invented fascinating sounds with mutes.

1928

Armstrong recorded "West End Blues," singing and playing with whimsy and lyricism. Aspiring musicians all around the United States fell in love with it.

1920S AND 1930S

When Armstrong became a hit with his Hot Five and Hot Seven bands on recordings, the record companies began to com-

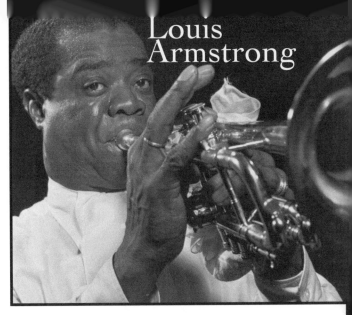

Louis Armstrong

pete against each other by signing other trumpeters and cornetists. The Brunswick label signed *Gladys "Jabbo" Smith*, a Georgia-born, blues-rooted trumpeter and singer, who was popular in Chicago. Victor signed New Orleans-born *Henry "Red" Allen*, who had immersed himself in Armstrong's style.

Jimmie Noone led his own band at the Apex club in Chicago. *Jonah Jones*, who would become known in Cab Calloway's band in the 1940s and then lead his own group, heard Armstrong at the Vendome Theater, where Armstrong had become a star of the orchestra, and decided to devote his own life to playing trumpet. Many young musicians were influenced in the same way by hearing Armstrong.

Roy Eldridge first learned to play cornet from *Rex Stewart*, who played in Duke Ellington's band. In the 1920s, Eldridge thought Armstrong's sound was too rough, and he preferred to take tenor saxophonist *Coleman Hawkins* and alto saxophonist

Benny Carter as his role models. Hawkins had, in fact, developed his style from Armstrong's sound; he was the leading saxophonist of this era, when the tenor became king of the saxes in jazz. So, indirectly, Eldridge also learned from Armstrong in the 1920s. By the 1930s, Eldridge realized how great Armstrong was and studied his style and technique seriously.

Benny Carter, *Johnny Hodges* (in Duke's band), and *Willie Smith*—all alto sax players—were important role models in this era, even though the tenor saxophone was more popular.

Eldridge joined Teddy Hill's band and impressed a budding young trumpeter from South Carolina. That talented youngster, *Dizzy Gillespie*, would become a jazz revolutionary in the 1940s.

Tennessee-born trumpeter *Doc Cheatham* filled in twice for Armstrong at the Vendome Theater in Chicago. Cheatham went on to have the longest career of any trumpeter in jazz.

Bix Beiderbecke, a white cornetist from Davenport, Iowa, learned to play jazz from recordings by a white group called the Original Dixieland Jazz Band. He began leading his own group, the Wolverines, in Chicago. An instinctive genius, Beiderbecke influenced Chicago cornetist *Jimmy McPartland*, trumpeter *Bobby Hackett*, and the exciting, creative, and rough-hewn clarinetist *Pee Wee Russell*, all very notable players and stylists.

Beiderbecke played with several big bands, among them Paul Whiteman's, and became friends with his bandmate, saxophonist *Frankie Trumbauer*, who taught Bix how to read music. Beiderbecke, admired by Armstrong, died young of alcoholism in 1931, leaving behind recordings of great beauty.

Among the most important tenor saxophonists of the era, after Coleman Hawkins, were *Ben Webster, Don Byas, Herschel Evans*, and *Lester Young*. Evans and Young played together in William "Count" Basie's band in the 1930s. Evans, with his big, swinging, outgoing southwestern style, died young. Young had a small, soft-toned, lyrical style, and there was a sophistication and modernity to his sound. He eventually said that he was particularly influenced by Frankie Trumbauer, as well as several important singers, including Frank Sinatra.

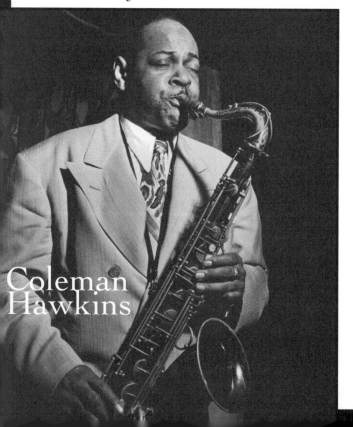

Coleman Hawkins

1938

Clarinetist **Benny Goodman** led a landmark jazz concert on January 16, 1938, at Carnegie Hall, with trumpeters **Ziggy Elman, Pee Wee Erwin, Bunny Berigan**, and **Harry James**. Also in the concert were baritone saxophonist **Harry Carney**, altoist **Johnny Hodges**, and trumpeter **Cootie Williams**, all from Duke Ellington's band, and Lester Young and trumpeter **Buck Clayton** from Count Basie's band.

1939

Coleman Hawkins recorded a classic version of "Body and Soul," against which all other saxophonists measured themselves. He was voted best tenor saxophonist in the world in a *Down Beat* magazine poll. Nevertheless, Lester Young's style was having a greater influence on young players. His slow, languid sound and coolness eclipsed Hawkins's big, earthy sound. Young's phrasing and rhythmic qualities predicted the coming revolution in jazz.

EARLY 1940S

Lester Young was nicknamed the "Prez" (president of the tenor saxophone) by his friend, singer Billie Holiday. Prez influenced many young tenor players, including **Dexter Gordon**, who would become noted for his great tone and fluidity, and **Illinois Jacquet**, with his big southwestern sound. Young was also a model for the stars of the 1940s, 1950s, and 1960s — **Stan Getz, Zoot Sims, Lee Konitz, Sonny Rollins, John Coltrane**, and many more.

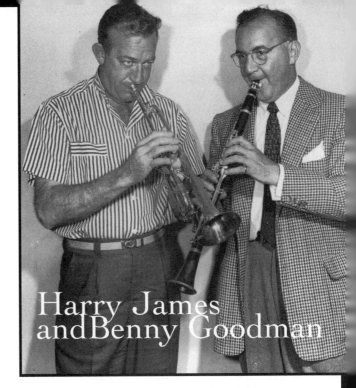

Harry James and Benny Goodman

Prez's tone, phrasing, melodic gifts, sweetness and bittersweetness, and long, flowing lines formed a bridge between the feeling and technique of the swing era and the bebop and post-bebop eras.

Trumpeter **Dizzy Gillespie**, traveling with Cab Calloway's band, met young alto saxophonist **Charlie "Bird" Parker** in Kansas City, Missouri. Both were experimenting with harmonies and began working together on modernizing jazz's harmonies and rhythms. Through the first half of the 1940s, they worked hard with other young musicians to develop their own style — a new language — for jazz. One of its hallmarks was the flatted fifth, which gave jazz a more plaintive, emotionally expressive sound. The press called the style bebop, probably because of the scat sounds the musicians used to name the songs as they were being rehearsed and developed, and also because some of the drum rhythms sounded choppy, like the word "bebop" itself. Bebop sounded strangely atonal and aggressive in those days, and its creators struggled to win fans.

THE BIG BAND ERA

Many of the important band leaders of the swing era, such as *Benny Goodman, Artie Shaw*, and *Woody Herman*, played clarinet. They won popularity polls in the United States. African-American musicians in Duke Ellington's band won polls in Europe. Racial prejudice may have been one reason for this division. Another was the repertoire—Duke's band played all his compositions, while other swing-era bands played pop tunes.

Count Basie's horn players established themselves as influential musicians in his blues-based, brassy-sounding powerhouse of a group. Among the important players with Basie from the 1930s into the 1950s were trumpeters *Buck Clayton* and *Harry "Sweets" Edison* in the early group, trombonist *Benny Powell*, fluegelhornist, trumpeter, and arranger *Thad Jones*, and saxophonists *Frank Wess* and *Frank Foster*.

A progressive group called *The Four Brothers* formed in Woody Herman's band—tenor sax players *Zoot Sims*, *Stan Getz*, and *Herbie Stewart*, and baritone saxophonist *Serge Chaloff*. Later, tenorists *Al Cohn* and *Gene Ammons* would join the group. Saxophonist *Jimmy Giuffre* wrote arrangements for it.

Tommy Dorsey, who led his own band, was a fine trombonist. From watching him play, Frank Sinatra learned about phrasing. In Tommy's band were *Buddy DeFranco*, a clarinet star, and trumpeter *Charlie Shavers*.

The big band era ended in the late 1940s. By the 1950s, the clarinet had become an outmoded instrument in jazz, although the reputations of Benny Goodman and Buddy DeFranco would never diminish. The soprano saxophone was becoming more popular. In the post-World War II era, as the world became much more complicated and international competition between the Soviet Union and the United States posed the threat of nuclear war, the musical tastes of Americans changed. Bebop, which was far more sophisticated, moody, fiery, and even aggressive than swing, increasingly intrigued the public. The beboppers focused on playing complicated figures at fast tempos.

Dizzy Gillespie

1945

Bebop recordings done in February and May made Dizzy and Bird famous. Sessions included the songs "Groovin' High," "Dizzy Atmosphere," "All the Things You Are," "Shaw Nuff," " Lover Man," "Salt Peanuts," and "Hot House." Dizzy began to achieve fame as a leader of small groups, then of a big band.

LATE 1940S

Dizzy and Bird led their own groups; because of Bird's unreliability they played together only on rare occasions. Dizzy often used altoist *Sonny Stitt*, who had modeled himself after Bird. Bird hired the young trumpeter *Miles Davis*, who idolized Dizzy. Dizzy, who could play in a very high register at breakneck speeds, told Miles that he didn't play the high

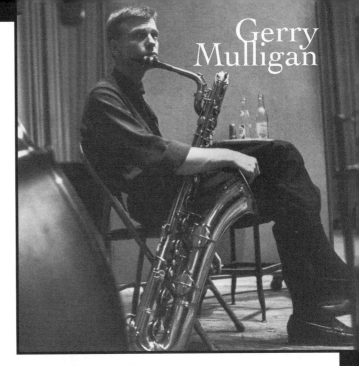

Gerry Mulligan

notes well because he didn't hear music in that high register. But with Bird's group, Miles began establishing the strength of his haunting, eerie tone in the trumpet's middle register.

Miles, working with pianist-arranger Gil Evans, baritone saxophonist *Gerry Mulligan*, and others, recorded *Birth of the Cool* in 1947. The group's ideas were based in part on big-band leader Claude Thornhill's cool-sounding, laid-back work, which Evans had arranged. *Birth of the Cool* was released in 1953. The nine players on the album included young alto saxophonists *Lee Konitz* and *Stan Getz*.

EARLY 1950S

In 1953, Dizzy and Bird played with pianist Bud Powell, bassist Charles Mingus, and drummer Max Roach at Massey Hall in Toronto, Canada, for a concert billed as "The Greatest Jazz

Miles Davis

Concert Ever." The recording of the concert became a jazz classic.

Around the same time, **Gerry Mulligan** went to live in California, where he formed a pianoless quartet that included trumpeter and singer **Chet Baker**. Playing a laid-back music supposedly inspired by California's beach culture and relaxed lifestyle, the quartet had a roaring success with its cool, dreamy music. Baker had a soft, haunting, tender sound and a lyrical style.

More cool music came from the lyrical alto saxophonist **Paul Desmond** in pianist Dave Brubeck's quartet. Desmond, influenced by Lester Young and Bird, played with airiness, fluidity, and ease, and he made Brubeck's group really swing. Desmond wrote the quartet's major hit, "Take Five," with its repetitious theme lifted by Desmond's solo.

In 1955, Bird died at age thirty-four from his addictions to heroin and alcohol.

LATE 1950S

Dizzy was chosen to take a big band on several very successful State Department tours. His career became stable, and his future was assured. Dizzy took along a young female trombonist and arranger, **Melba Liston**, on these tours. She was not only a great player, but she could also write music very well. Her dual abilities made her a valued part of many important jazz groups, which ordinarily did not hire female players in those days.

Miles Davis formed his own group in 1955 and began recording, establishing himself as the most influential modern jazz player. In addition to his sound and the talents of the wonderful musicians he hired, he concentrated on using modes—themes, or sequences of notes—instead of chords as the basis for improvisation. He felt that jazz, during the bebop revolution, had become too thick with chords. One of his sidemen was tenor saxophonist **John Coltrane**, who had started on alto under the influence of Bird but switched to tenor to try to establish his own sound and style. Coltrane loved the work of Lester Young and Coleman Hawkins. He played a deluge of sixteenth notes, which made a fine foil for Miles's calm, precise trumpet. Coltrane also led his own groups.

Paul Desmond and the Dave Brubeck quartet

HEIRS OF BEBOP

Saxophonist **James Moody**, who played with Dizzy's bands from 1948 to 1952, went to Europe and improvised a song, "Moody's Mood for Love," based on the chords of "I'm in the Mood for Love." He became very successful in Europe and the United States.

Young trumpeter **Theodore "Fats" Navarro** had a beautiful tone and great lyrical gifts. Unfortunately, he died young from illnesses brought on by self-neglect. Another highly regarded young trumpeter, **Clifford Brown**, also died young in a car accident on the way to a gig.

Trumpeter **Red Rodney** became a protégé of Bird. unfortunately, Red was a heroin addict, like Bird, and spent time in jail. But he recovered and reestablished his career later in life.

Tenorist **Dexter Gordon**, alto and tenor saxophonist **Charles McPherson**, and altoists **Julian "Cannonball" Adderley** and **Charles Mariano**, among others, became musical heirs of Dizzy and Bird. Adderley began leading his own group in 1953, recording such hits as the soulful, blues-rooted "Mercy, Mercy, Mercy." He concentrated on the blues roots of jazz, and critics called it a "hard bop" style. His younger brother, trumpeter **Nat Adderley**, played in his own group.

Many young saxophonists, having fallen under Bird's spell, chose to play alto instead of tenor. His heirs, no matter what instrument they played, often went on to enjoy distinguished careers. **J. J.**

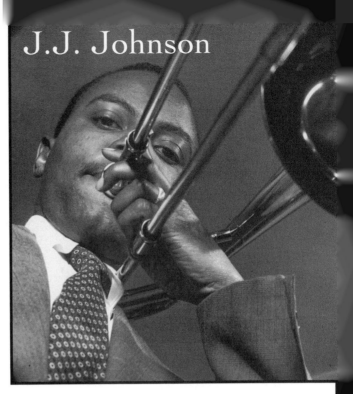

J.J. Johnson

Johnson, for example, became the most important modern trombonist to mature during the bebop era, and he has continued to command respect.

Many important horn players matured in a hard bop group led by drummer Art Blakey, among them trumpeters **Lee Morgan**, **Freddie Hubbard**, and **Woody Shaw** and tenor saxophonist Hank Mobley. Shaw later played in groups with tenor saxophonist **Joe Henderson** and trombonist **Steve Turre**. Turre developed into a formidable musician and group leader.

Other notable horn players of the period were saxophonist **Wardell Gray**, who died young under mysterious circumstances; the great trombone balladeer **Al Grey**; bluesy alto saxophonist **Lou Donaldson**, who became famous for playing in a funky style; tenorist **Johnny Griffin**, who had a light, airy style; **Yusef Lateef**, who became especially attracted to and involved in the music of foreign cultures; and altoist **John Handy**, who played with bassist Charles Mingus and also became well known for an album taped at the Monterey Jazz Festival in the 1960s.

Altoist **Chris Woods**, an heir of bebop, became a striking soloist and a great duo partner for trumpeter/fluegelhornist/ singer **Clark Terry**. Terry distinguished himself in many groups as a player and leader throughout his long career. **Phil Woods**, a fiery altoist under the influence of Bird, and **Rahsaan Roland Kirk**, a blind, gifted multi-instrumentalist, were two more praiseworthy individualists.

Trumpeter and fluegelhornist **Art Farmer** led a ten-piece ensemble with saxophonist **Benny Golson**. Trumpeter **Joe Wilder** established a career in jazz and in Broadway orchestras and studios. Trumpeter and fluegelhornist **Thad Jones**, out of Basie's band, played in the studios and founded an innovative big band that played his own arrangements in the 1960s. Saxophonists **Gigi Gryce**, **Jimmy Heath**, and **Lucky Thompson** were very admired musicians. Heath has led a number of popular groups though the years.

LATE 1950S AND INTO THE 1960S

Bebop became passé; that is, although its influence endured, its popularity was eclipsed by new sounds, extensions of the ideas put in motion by bebop. Miles Davis's sound was virtually a new aesthetic, a new artistic goal. Miles was playing a softer, slower-paced, more melodic music.

In 1959, Davis recorded *Kind of Blue*, a modal classic. John Coltrane played on the recording, then formed his own band, with which he recorded *Giant Steps*, another significant album in the modal style.

Among the young, strong, modern horn players who passed through Davis's groups in the 1950s and 1960s were tenorist **George Coleman** on the albums *Four and More* and *My Funny Valentine* and multi-reeds player **Wayne Shorter** on the album *Miles Smiles*. Shorter became known particularly as a composer and soprano and tenor saxophonist.

In the late 1950s, it appeared as if tenor saxophonist **Sonny Rollins** would lead his generation on his instrument. He had the virility of Coleman Hawkins, the swing and airiness of Lester Young, and the progressive ideas of Charlie Parker. He also had

Clark Terry

great stamina. But John Coltrane came along and surprised Rollins. Coltrane not only had drive and a superb sound, but his music clearly reflected his spiritual quest as a musician. That spirituality established him as the colossus of the tenor saxophone by the 1960s. In the last years of his life, he began playing free jazz—music free of traditional form. Rollins remained a very important artist. He also has outlived Coltrane by at least three decades and is still going strong, playing in the mainstream tradition at sold-out concerts. Many of his compositions, such as "St. Thomas," have become great jazz standards.

FREE JAZZ

On bass clarinet, alto saxophone, and flute, *Eric Dolphy* became a very important player, influenced first by Bird. Dolphy started out with free jazz, improvising neither on chords nor modes but on ideas of his own devising. Moving from the West Coast to New York in the late 1950s, he joined the free jazz group of alto saxophonist **Ornette Coleman** for a performance that stunned the jazz world in 1959. Dolphy then went on to play with bassist Charles Mingus in experimental groups. Then John Coltrane hired Dolphy. Dolphy was recognized as a genius by many jazz musicians. But as a revolutionary, he had a very difficult time earning a living in the United States, and he lived in extreme poverty. In uncertain health, with a chronic diabetic condition, he went to work in Europe in the mid-

Sonny Rollins

1960s. He died there, probably from an overdose of insulin.

The music of Ornette Coleman was totally liberated from the restrictions of chords or any other proscribed musical form. His band members improvised collectively (that is, at the same time), no one soloed, and everyone played a different line in a different tempo and key. A close associate of Coleman's was trumpeter **Don Cherry**. Coleman provided leadership for the small free jazz movement among the horn players. Miles Davis thought Coleman was crazy, and many others thought the same thing for a while. Coleman and his musicians emphasized sound over form. Free jazz sounded like pure screaming at times. In time, others saw the brilliance of Coleman's ideas, and free jazz would influence even mainstream players in the long run.

In 1957, Gunther Schuller, a classical French horn player, teacher, composer, and eminent critic, said that form could evolve out of the material presented. It was a valid concept for modern life. Nevertheless, free jazz artists did not easily win friends, fans, or financial support for their work. They persisted bravely. An important group to evolve in the free jazz movement was *The World Saxophone Quartet*, with *Anthony Braxton, Julius Hemphill, Oliver Lake*, and the witty baritone saxophonist *Hamiett Bluiett*.

1960S

At the same time that free jazz was developing, jazz-rock fusion music, combining electric and acoustic instruments, kept jazz before the public. Miles Davis started the trend in 1969 with his recording *Bitches Brew*, the first jazz-rock fusion album. Fluegelhornist *Chuck Mangione*'s fusion group had a pop hit with the song "Feels So Good." *Weather Report*, co-led by composer and saxophonist *Wayne Shorter* and keyboardist Joe Zawinul, presented a happy blend of artistically interesting and commercially appealing music.

John
Coltrane

1960S TO 1970S

The jazz world split into two distinct factions. In the 1960s, rock ruled the pop music world, while free jazz drove people out of the clubs, especially fans of traditional, melodic jazz. Jazz musicians on all the instruments scurried to find work. Some disappeared into studios in New York and Los Angeles, and others played rock; still more went to Europe to find work as acoustic jazz artists.

1980

Wynton Marsalis, a very talented young trumpeter from New Orleans, backed by Gunther Schuller, was admitted to Juilliard. He also began playing with Art Blakey's Jazz Messengers. Able to play both jazz and classical music, Wynton was signed by Columbia Records. He had such great artistic and commercial success that he helped spawn a renaissance of the public's interest in jazz. Legions of young musicians on all the instruments got the chance to perform, record, and lead groups. Older musicians, too, had their careers rejuvenated.

1990S

Among the new generation of thousands of jazz musicians, the most famous players and composers have been trumpeters—Wynton Marsalis, who became director of the Lincoln Center Jazz Program; Dizzy Gillespie's protégé *Jon Faddis*, director of the Carnegie Hall Jazz Band; and *Terence Blanchard*, composer of scores for Spike Lee's films. Still younger trumpeters such as

Ornette Coleman

Roy Hargrove, Philip Harper, and *Nicholas Payton*, found themselves being fussed over more than the talented players of other instruments. These trumpeters are essentially mainstream players clinging to their roots in the bebop and modal tradition.

Even free jazz players earned their share of respect and commercial success. Ornette Coleman, for example, received a MacArthur award (often called the "genius award"). Mainstream musicians now play some of his compositions. And jazz-rock fusion players and mellow jazz players also had their followings. Women horn players finally began to have their talents recognized, too; they began to get gigs and even recording contracts.

Jazz has split into many factions; it continues to grow and take new forms.

SIX

THE ORBIT OF MILES DAVIS

*I*f it were possible to know in advance exactly what type of music or which songs the public is going to like, musicians could make recordings and become millionaires with ease. But the public is fickle and unpredictable. At the start of the 1950s, people decided they wanted a softer sound than bebop. And Miles Davis began his ascent to superstardom. He would become one of the most artistically influential jazz musicians and rock/jazz fusion group leaders of the century.

In Bird's groups, Miles had distinguished himself primarily for the beauty of his tonal quality. Gil Evans, an arranger and pianist who had written for the Claude Thornhill big band, recognized Miles's potential for introducing a new sound into jazz. Where the beboppers had communicated their emotions and ideas by fiery playing, Miles could express profound feeling by sustaining pure, melodic lines in the middle register of the trumpet.

Gil Evans was about seventeen when he led his first jazz orchestra in Stockton, California, in the early 1930s. He revered his Louis Armstrong and Duke Ellington records. He went to New York in the 1930s and met Benny Goodman and Fletcher Henderson, two more of his heroes. He led a band for the Bob Hope radio show, went into the army, and, after World War II, wrote bebop-style arrangements for Claude Thornhill's band.

In 1946, coming off the road, Gil established his studio on West 52nd Street, where he virtually held court. Musicians such as pianist George

Russell, Charlie Parker, Miles Davis, and baritone saxophonist Gerry Mulligan—an interracial group—visited or stayed with him. "And they created the birth of the cool and the whole new music there," said his widow, Anita Evans. "So in New York in the 1940s, Gil got to hang with the people he admired the most on the planet, and that was it. He never left that realm."[1]

Miles Dewey Davis III was born on May 26, 1926, in Alton, Illinois, and grew up in East St. Louis, then a quiet, segregated little community. His father, a dentist, owned a house in East St. Louis with a small back porch, where Miles and his friends used to listen to the big bands on the radio. The bands were Miles's first great musical influence.

Miles idolized his father and took lessons from Dr. Davis's radical views on race. Dr. Davis disdained Abraham Lincoln and the NAACP and instead championed Marcus Garvey and his ideas about separation of the races. Even so, Miles would later give one of his greatest concerts at Lincoln Center in New York on February 12, 1964, to raise money to help register African-Americans to vote in Mississippi and Louisiana. That was clearly a bid for integration. But sometimes Miles talked about his great antipathy for whites or white supremacy, which he seemed to feel were the same thing. His friends thought Miles was a very proud, complicated man.

In high school, his marching band teacher told Miles not to play with vibrato on purpose: "You'll shake when you get old," the teacher said. He asked Miles to play the trumpet with a more straightforward tone to bring out "the pure sound of the instrument," Miles later recalled.[2]

Older trumpeters in town advised him about his embouchure—the way he used his mouth—and mouthpieces. Miles studied with the first chair trumpet player in the St. Louis Symphony Orchestra. Clark Terry, who was a little older than Miles and living in East St. Louis, influenced Miles's sense of fashion. Miles loved clothes. Even as a teenager, he loved wearing shirts with collars so stiff that he couldn't move his neck. People would recall they sometimes complimented Miles on the way he sounded, and he would say, "Never mind that. How'd I look?" Miles would become known for his hip, cool way of dressing and behaving.

As a teenager, he liked the sophisticated music of New York as well as the sound of the blues and spirituals popular in the Midwest and South. Some people would always hear the blues roots in Miles's playing and tone. He could use a single note to incredible advantage, much the way the southern and midwestern blues singers and guitarists did.

At age seventeen, he married his girlfriend, and they had two children. She encouraged him to try to get a job with Eddie Randall's Blue Devils band in East St. Louis. Randall would recall that he was attracted to Miles's sound, though Miles still had a great deal to learn about playing the trumpet.

In 1944, the Billy Eckstine band passed through town. Miles loved it so much that he learned every trumpeter's part by ear. When a trumpeter in the band got sick, Miles took his place. The Eckstine men weren't very impressed by Miles's playing. But Miles was hypnotized by the band and knew he wanted to play music for his life's work. Over his mother's objections, and with his father's blessings and tuition money, Miles set off to study at Juilliard in New York.

He loved the fast pace of New York City, the music, the clothes, the slangy language he heard. He didn't love Juilliard, however, and instead went to hear the young beboppers at Minton's in Harlem and the Onyx and the Three Deuces on 52nd Street. He spent time with trumpeter Freddie Webster. Miles brought Freddie with him to his first recording session, a date with "Rubberlegs" Williams, a well-known 52nd Street entertainer. Miles got through the date, though he played without distinction. His confidence and technique kept growing. He sounded much better when he recorded a year later with the fine baritone singer Earl Coleman.

In 1944, Dizzy became Miles's main mentor. Miles was unable to play in a high register, and Dizzy told him it was because he wasn't hearing the notes way up there. Miles heard the same chords that Dizzy did, but in a lower register. When Miles asked about a note Dizzy played, Dizzy showed him the chord on the piano and said, "Here's the note."

That was a great help to Miles, whose harmonic concept would eventually make a big contribution to jazz. By 1955, Miles had a knowledge of harmony and his own great technique. He was able to take Dizzy's

Miles Davis began to develop his haunting sound in Charlie "Bird" Parker's band in the 1940s.

introduction to Thelonious Monk's "Round Midnight" and stress certain notes, cut out others, and create a much more taut, atmospheric, eerie piece than Dizzy played.

Miles was already cultivating his sound in the mid-1940s. In 1945, when he played his first recording dates with Bird, Miles didn't have the technique to measure up to the master beboppers. But his tone was already evident.

Miles led his own group on records for the first time in 1947, with Bird on the date. Miles played his own song, "Donna Lee." Both Gerry Mulligan and Gil Evans listened admiringly to the beboppers, but especially to Miles. Evans wrote an arrangement of "Donna Lee" for the Thornhill orchestra. Miles, in turn, was struck by Evans's work and became drawn to a softer, slower-paced, more melodic sound than the beboppers cultivated. By 1949, Miles and Gil were collaborating in earnest.

Evans, Mulligan, and Miles organized a nine-piece band and in 1947 recorded *Birth of the Cool* for Capitol Records. It would not be released until 1953. Mulligan would recall, "Miles and I had tastes in common. Both of us loved the Thornhill band, and the way Gil used the orchestration flabbergasted us. It didn't seem revolutionary, it seemed logical. We used instruments with timbres that matched as much as they could — one of each. In the high section was a trumpet and an alto, in the middle a trombone and French horn, and in the low section a baritone and tuba. Those basic colors to work with." Miles noted, "We started getting it together — the Claude Thornhill sound with us." And there was the rhythm section of piano, bass, and drums. The nonet, which also included tenor saxophonists Lee Konitz and Stan Getz, arranger Johnny Carisi, drummer Max Roach, and pianist John Lewis, had a big-band sound with the freedom of a small group.

When Miles and Mulligan walked down Fifth Avenue together — Mulligan tall, thin, and red-haired, Miles very dark-skinned, small, and compact — people stared at them. Miles was annoyed by the attention. In early 1949, he went to work in France, where racism was less apparent. Miles loved that social freedom.

100

In France, he met the famous existential philosopher Jean Paul Sartre and painter Pablo Picasso. Miles sat with them in cafés, talking until the wee hours of the morning. And he fell in love with French singer Juliette Greco. Miles liked being with her, despite their language barrier. He made a better living in Europe than in America. He recorded for a film soundtrack in Paris at a time when Americans had not yet started using jazz in movies.

Juliet and his friends tried to persuade Miles to stay in Paris. "But I had to finish the *Birth of the Cool* stuff," Miles said. He needed the stimulation of American and African-American music and society.

At home, his first marriage was over. And even though he had seen the great damage Bird had caused himself with heroin, Miles began using drugs. Miles had signed to record for Prestige Records and did many dates for the company. But because he was so addicted, he pawned his horn for money for drugs and tried to borrow horns for gigs. He became a pimp and a thief to raise money for heroin. He looked a mess. One day, Max Roach told Miles that he was looking good and stuffed $100 in his pocket. That's when Miles realized he had to stop using drugs. He went to a farm that his father owned and cured himself by quitting cold turkey.

In the mid-1950s, he returned healthy to New York, a star with a proud, even arrogant attitude. He left Prestige in 1954 for a better contract with Columbia. In performances he rebelliously turned his back on audiences. And he was clearly one of the greatest trumpet stylists. His eerie sound set him above everyone else. A British critic called it "the sound of loneliness."

But it was loneliness buoyed up by pensiveness and self-assertion. He had a lofty quality, as if he were playing from a great height down to people. He thought for himself. He didn't sound as if he was pining away for anything or anybody. He stood apart and above everyone else. And he had the odd habit of pointing the bell of his trumpet at the floor when he played. That was a difficult position to play in, other trumpeters noticed.

He also refused to play endless sets in a single night with only twenty-minute breaks. He became known as an outspoken, arrogant man, who related to people primarily through music. His *Birth of the Cool* collaboration with Evans paved the way for even greater artistic successes with the melodic album *Miles Ahead* in 1957, with a nineteen-piece band. Miles's interpretation of George Gershwin's *Porgy and Bess* in 1958 is a brilliant and relentlessly beautiful album. His album *Sketches of Spain*, recorded in 1959, became his most popular one in the 1960s. But some critics have thought *Porgy and Bess* and *Miles Smiles* were his best albums. He had legions of fans who adored his moods, solos, and ideas.

By 1955, Miles had formed a quintet of great soloists. Tenor saxophonist John Coltrane was in the group, providing a foil with his sheets of sound—a deluge of sixteenth notes—for the pristine beauty of Miles's calm, precise trumpet. Alto saxophonist Julian "Cannonball" Adderley also joined Miles's group. Both Adderley and Coltrane would eventually lead their own important and popular groups.

In Miles's group, Coltrane was increasing his understanding of harmonies. When Miles failed to keep him on in 1957, Coltrane briefly went to work for Thelonious Monk and learned even more about harmonies. He returned to Miles's group to record the modal classic *Kind of Blue* in 1959. It was the first entire album to use the modal approach.

A mode is a sequence of notes in a whole-step, half-step pattern that establishes a tonality—a keynote to which the whole work eventually gravitates. Miles decided to use modes as a basis for his compositions, because he felt jazz had become too dense with chords. With modes, there were fewer chords and more choices about what to do with them. Instead of relying on great numbers of chords, improvisers had to be more inventive.

Kind of Blue became one of the most beloved and influential modern jazz albums. Then Coltrane formed his own group in 1959 and recorded one of his early modal masterpieces, *Giant Steps*. He concentrated completely on modal music for a while.

Miles formed groups with young, strong, modern musicians throughout the 1960s. And he underwent many changes, becoming more virtuosic, able to play anything he wanted to, even acquitting himself regally in a high register. *Four and More* and *My Funny Valentine*, two albums that came out of a Congress of Racial Equality concert to benefit voter registration work in 1964, showed off the traditional tenor saxophonist George Coleman. Miles was empowered by this group, particularly his brilliant rhythm section of pianist Herbie Hancock, bassist Ron Carter, and drummer Tony Williams, and he reached great heights of melodic and rhythmic virtuosity. One of his finest albums, *Miles Smiles*, done in 1966, included the adventurous saxophonist Wayne Shorter.

Shorter, a masterful improviser, came from Art Blakey's Jazz Messengers and stayed with Miles only a little while. He was destined to lead his own groups, and he became particularly admired as a composer. Blakey always required his young sidemen to compose. He told them they had to write for posterity, immortality, and the financial security that royalties could provide. When Blakey's young protégés became ready, in his estimation, he told them to leave his band and lead their own groups. Then he took on new young talent. He had a great knack for finding wonderful horn players.

TRANSITIONS

In 1967, Miles recorded *Nefertiti*, then *Filles de Killimanjaro*, on which pianist Chick Corea replaced Herbie Hancock. In 1969, Miles underwent another transition, from jazz to jazz/rock fusion with electronic instruments. His album *In a Silent Way* started the transition, and in the same year *Bitches Brew* established the new style. By that time, acoustic jazz had become a financial liability to recording companies. Jazz had lost its hold on the public. In his own sweet way, Miles rescued jazz from economic oblivion by combining acoustic and electronic instruments in one group.

Rock music was dominating the country's popular music scene. Some former big-band instrumentalists worked in studio orchestras. Others had to leave the music business altogether, because they couldn't read music well enough to work in the studios, or they didn't have the right connections to get jobs. Still other players went to Europe and found work in an atmosphere where American jazz musicians were revered. They taught Europeans to play better. And some jazz musicians went to California studios, searching for ways to call attention to themselves and play or write music that would appeal to the public.

Gerry Mulligan went to California and began working and recording with a new small group. For one recording session, he had a pianist. Soon he decided to play without one, working instead with a young trumpeter, Chet Baker, drummer Chico Hamilton, and a bassist. This quartet played intense but calming music supposedly inspired by the laid-back ambiance of California's beach-oriented culture. With this sound, Mulligan, the leader, and Baker, his handsome sideman with an exquisite tone, had a roaring, unexpected success.

Their music was dreamy — cool. It may have been nurtured by California's atmosphere or by the Gil Evans/Miles Davis collaboration that included Gerry and his arrangements. In any case, freed of the piano, Gerry and Chet played intricate counterpoint to each other. And Gerry's future as a major figure in jazz history was assured.

Chet Baker became a tragic figure — a hopeless drug addict, in and out of jails and clinics. But he accomplished the miracle of always performing as a first-rate trumpeter and singer with a soft, haunting, tender sound and a lyrical style. He left a legacy of exquisite recordings that gave no hint of his torturous life, in which he disappointed everyone who became intimately involved with him.

Alto saxophonist Paul Desmond joined pianist Dave Brubeck in another experimental group. Brubeck stressed a blending of European classical music with jazz. He played with a heavy touch and achieved his best moments when he played fascinating separate rhythms with his right and left hands. Desmond, influenced by Lester Young, Charlie Parker, and other saxophonists with a cool, modern sound, played beautiful melodies with airiness, fluidity, and ease. Desmond's lightness and superior tone and feeling helped the Brubeck group achieve stardom in the jazz world.

By the end of the 1950s, Brubeck's group had several hits, in particular a monotonous, repetitive, easy-to-hum song called "Take Five," written

Alto saxophonist Cannonball Adderley had a popular, soulful group which had a hit with the song "Mercy, Mercy, Mercy" among his many beautiful recordings.

Trumpeter Chet Baker, a perennial bad boy, always played and sang with a dreamy, pure sound.

by Desmond, who plays a hypnotic, melodic solo. The tune is still played all the time, on the radio and in commercials.

Cannonball Adderley was under the influence of Bird and earlier altoists and deeply affected by John Coltrane's work in Miles's group. He led his own blues-rooted, soulful, fiery group, with his brother Nat on trumpet and cornet. Cannonball's quintet, which began recording in 1959, had several hits, including "Mercy, Mercy, Mercy," written by the group's keyboardist, Joe Zawinul. Joe would later co-found Weather Report, an extremely popular jazz/rock fusion group, with Wayne Shorter.

Cannonball, a huge man with voracious appetites and physical complications from them, died at age forty-six of a stroke. He had been one of the finest of the "hard bop" leaders, along with Art Blakey and pianist/composer Horace Silver—musicians who left behind the convolutions of early bebop. They played instead in a straightforward style and sought inspiration in the blues-rooted music of the African-American heritage. The name "hard bop" may have come from Blakey's hard-hitting drum style.

Miles maintained the haunting beauty of his tone during his forays into jazz/rock fusion. But he confused and alienated jazz fans devoted to acoustic music. His bands became very loud and extremely electric, throbbing with appeal to fans of rock. He said his music delighted him. He couldn't think of anything that would bore him more than playing the old music that had so distinguished his groups in the 1950s and 1960s.

But a strange thing happened in the summer of 1991. He went to the jazz festival at Montreux, Switzerland, where he played in an acoustic jazz orchestra directed by Quincy Jones. (Jones, who began as a trumpeter, discovered his true strength lay in arranging and conducting. He became one of the first African-American composers and arrangers in the studios, and by the 1990s, he would be as famous as many of the musicians whose recordings he produced.) Most of the tunes were Miles's collaborations with Gil Evans, who had died in 1988. The exquisite music Quincy and Miles made together at Montreux was captured on a video and on the album *Miles & Quincy Live at Montreux*. A few months later, on September 28, 1991, Miles Davis died.

106

SEVEN

OTHER IMPORTANT HORN PLAYERS OF THE 1950S AND 1960S

*T*here were scores of other fine sidemen and group leaders playing reed and brass instruments in the 1950s and 1960s. They weren't innovators like Armstrong, Dizzy, Bird, Miles, and John Coltrane, but they won respect as exceptional stylists with unique sounds. Their work enriched jazz, which was becoming increasingly diversified.

Here is a brief survey of some of the significant trumpet and saxophone players of the era.

TRUMPETERS

Theodore "Fats" Navarro: Fats replaced Dizzy Gillespie as lead trumpeter in Billy Eckstine's band, then worked as a sideman and an occasional leader in small groups, particularly with pianist Lennie Tristano, a cool jazz guru. Fats rivaled Dizzy as a technician. For his sweet, brilliant tone and smooth style, Fats was peerless. But he ruined his health with heroin, contracted tuberculosis, and died at age twenty-six in 1950.

Clifford Brown: Charlie Parker, Dizzy Gillespie, and Fats Navarro served as role models for Clifford "Brownie" Brown. He recorded with Tadd Dameron, Sonny Rollins, Art Blakey and the Jazz Messengers, and Max Roach, with whom he led a quintet, one of the best in jazz.

He was a brilliant trumpeter with everything to live for. He had a happy marriage and the jazz world's recognition of his full-bodied, vibrant, sweet, melodic sound and control. He played articulately at slow and fast tempos. He was respected for his clean lifestyle, and he exerted a good influence on others. But he died in an auto accident, on his way to a gig on a foggy night, when he was twenty-five years old. The song "I Remember Clifford" would always have a special meaning for jazz fans.

Lee Morgan: Morgan, who revered Clifford's style, worked with Dizzy Gillespie, Art Blakey, John Coltrane, and tenor saxophonist Hank Mobley. (Mobley played in the first Jazz Messengers group.) With Blakey, Lee Morgan emerged as an important, extroverted stylist. *The Sidewinder* is regarded as one of his best albums. In 1972, at age thirty-three, he died the way he played, with flamboyance—his girlfriend shot him at Slug's, a New York jazz club.

Freddie Hubbard: Born in 1938, and particularly influenced by Clifford Brown, Freddie joined Art Blakey's Jazz Messengers, which gave him the boost he needed to launch his own groups. He also played and recorded in a well-loved but short-lived group called V.S.O.P. He has played every imaginable jazz, jazz-related, and pop style, including experimental, free jazz with alto saxophonist Ornette Coleman, who seemed shocking and radical in the 1960s. Hubbard's performances are surprising, fascinating, and exciting. He knows how to command attention and stand out in any group of fine players.

Woody Shaw: In 1964, Shaw began an important part of his career at about age twenty when he went to work in Paris with notable expatriate

American musicians. Among them was tenor saxophonist Johnny Griffin. Shaw made the rounds of important groups, playing with pianists Horace Silver and McCoy Tyner, alto saxophonist Jackie McLean, drummer Max Roach, and tenor saxophonist Joe Henderson. Henderson gained praise and popularity in the 1990s, winning awards and top honors in critics polls for his albums and his performances.

In the mid-1970s, Woody co-led a group with drummer Louis Hayes and eventually with Dexter Gordon. He and Dexter played together for nearly the rest of Woody's life. Woody also led his own groups, with such excellent musicians as trombonist Steve Turre. Woody died in May 1989, a few months after a gruesome accident in a New York subway. He was a sweet, melodic, imaginative player. Despite his poor vision and poor health—he had diabetes—he left a rich legacy of records and songs.

SAXOPHONISTS

Tenor saxophonist **Stan Getz** was noted for his light sound and lyrical style, particularly moving on ballads. He worked with many legendary jazz musicians, including Jack Teagarden, Stan Kenton, Benny Goodman, Dizzy Gillespie, Sonny Stitt, and Woody Herman. In Herman's band, Getz became part of the Four Brothers.

He won renown for his fusion of jazz with Brazil's bossa nova. His recordings with guitarist Charlie Byrd and Brazilian singers Joao and Astrud Gilberto were commercial hits. Like Miles's music, they focused attention on jazz during the reign of rock. Getz died in his mid-60s in California in 1991. Donald Maggin's book *Stan Getz: A Life in Jazz* describes his wild life culminating in his heroic, dignified battle with cancer as he continued to work.

Tenorist **Dexter Gordon,** a native Californian and the son of a doctor, began playing in swing-era bands led by Lionel Hampton and Pops Armstrong. He then established himself as a striking player in bebop groups and worked with many outstanding musicians, such as saxophonist Wardell Gray, until the early 1960s. Dexter's life became plagued with

Trumpeter Fats Navarro rivaled Dizzy for technique and had a prettier sound, but Fats died too young to establish the major reputation he deserved.

Tenor saxophonist Stan Getz made his mark as a great lover and player of beautiful melodies, and he popularized the lovely sound of Brazilian music in the United States.

legal problems because of his drug addiction. (Musicians who had come from more humble circumstances and never used heroin took a dim view of Dexter's drug problem, thinking he didn't have a good excuse for it.)

He moved to Copenhagen, Denmark, where, despite his disorganization, he was a highly respected group leader and teacher. He played in major festivals and clubs in Europe and Japan for the next fifteen years. Returning to live in the United States, he was honored in various ways. For his acting in the 1986 movie *Round Midnight,* he received an Academy Award nomination.

Gordon was a pivotal figure, starting under the influence of the best swing-era tenorists, including Lester Young, Coleman Hawkins, and the outgoing Texas tenors. He then took in the lessons of Charlie Parker. With his beautiful tone and harmonic ideas, Dexter had a hypnotic effect on modernists such as tenorists Sonny Rollins and John Coltrane.

Alto saxophonist *Lou Donaldson* played with important figures in the swing and bebop eras, even Art Blakey's Jazz Messengers in the 1950s. After that he led his own groups in jazz and funk. An excellent singer, too, he is a very entertaining, blues-based artist.

Tenorist *Johnny Griffin*: Circulating in the jazz world in groups led by swing-era and bebop artists and the exuberant Texas tenor Arnett Cobb, Griffin eventually played with Art Blakey and Thelonious Monk. He then led a quintet with Eddie "Lockjaw" Davis, another tenor saxophonist who made an excellent foil for Griffin. Davis played in such a low register on his tenor that he sounded like a baritone player, while Griffin has a light, airy style. An important member of a highly regarded European band led by Kenny Clarke and Francy Boland, Griffin settled in France permanently.

Altoist *Lee Konitz:* Originally under the influence of Lester Young's concept on the tenor, Konitz became involved in Miles Davis's *Birth of the Cool* recordings. Throughout his life he has worked with experimentalists such as pianist and teacher Lennie Tristano, a guru for the cool school, and with other curious, searching, bebop-rooted modernists in the United States and Europe. He has a cool, smooth, vibrato-less approach and a distinctive style.

Tenorist *Yusef Lateef:* He began working in the swing era with some of the leading bands, played with Dizzy Gillespie around 1950, and then went back to school to study composition and flute. He converted to Islam (changing his name from William Evans) and became fascinated by the instruments of foreign cultures and Asian, Middle Eastern, and African music.

Altoist *John Handy:* A well-known college teacher living in San Francisco, Handy became especially noted for his performance at the Monterey Jazz Festival in 1965. He worked with basssist Charles Mingus in the 1960s and, in the 1980s, played with the highly praised orchestra performing and recording Mingus's *Epitaph*.

Altoist *Chris Woods:* This heir of bebop was a striking soloist as well as a companion for twenty years in a group with Clark Terry. They could play and sing incredibly complicated figures in exact unison.

Altoist *Phil Woods:* A graduate of Juilliard, he had gravitated to jazz and worked in swing-era and bebop groups and in the studios into the 1960s. He has lived in New York, Europe, and California, winning tributes everywhere for his fiery style. He grew up under the influence of Charlie Parker.

AND MORE

Multi-reeds player *Rahsaan Roland Kirk:* Many photographs show this courageous blind saxophonist playing two and even three instruments at once. A very gifted improviser, he pursued his lifelong interest in many instruments—probably more than any other jazz musician ever played. He worked with Charles Mingus, led his own groups, and in the 1970s agitated for more opportunities for African-American musicians. After suffering a stroke, he devised ways that allowed him to keep playing until his untimely death at age forty-one in 1977.

Trombonist *J. J. Johnson:* By the early 1940s, when he was playing in Benny Carter's orchestra, J. J. was recognized as the great new trombonist on the scene. He played frequently with the beboppers in the 1940s but suffered the same financial reverses that Dizzy did in the early 1950s. When he formed a group with trombonist Kai Winding, he gained greater acclaim and became known to a wider public. He performed, taught, and composed, working with Miles Davis and other well-known jazz players. He switched to the Los Angeles studio scene in the 1970s, then resumed an active playing career as jazz began a renaissance in the late 1970s.

There were other notable players in the 1950s and 1960s, among them *Art Farmer* and *Thad Jones* on trumpet and fluegelhorn; Jones eventually co-led his own superb band that played his compositions, including his masterpiece, "A Child Is Born." Trumpeter Kenny Dorham played with Blakey and then started a similar group, the Jazz Prophets. Saxophonists include *Gigi Gryce, Benny Golson,* and *Charlie Rouse,* who played with Monk and later became a leading light of a fine quartet called Sphere. Golson and Farmer led a well-known group called the Tentet for a while. Tenor saxophonist *Jimmy Heath* composed lovely songs. Another tenorist, *Lucky Thompson,* was a highly respected player who simply left the scene and gave up playing in the 1970s; friends said Thompson couldn't stand the pressures of the business. *Joe Wilder,* one of the most highly regarded contemporary trumpeters, undaunted by the demands of any jazz style from swing to bebop, has traveled back and forth between jazz bands and Broadway orchestra pits. *Paul Jeffrey,* Thelonious Monk's last tenor player, became a teacher at Duke University.

These many stylists contributed much to the sound of jazz, but for influence, nobody became more important than Miles Davis and the artistically and spiritually driven John Coltrane.

EIGHT

JOHN COLTRANE AND ERIC DOLPHY

A legendary anecdote in the jazz world: John Coltrane played very, very long pieces. Once he told Miles Davis that he didn't know how to shorten the songs. Miles replied, "Take the horn out of your mouth."

Coltrane rarely did. When he stayed at the Hotel Alvin in midtown Manhattan, New York-born trumpeter Johnny Parker recalled, Coltrane used to stand in the stairwell between floors, practicing for hours. When Coltrane played in clubs, he went backstage during the breaks between sets and kept practicing. He worked himself to death, and in the process he became one of the most inspirational musicians in jazz. Legions of horn players—and musicians on other instruments, too—committed themselves to careers in music after they heard Coltrane.

It was thought that Sonny Rollins would be the undisputed leader on tenor saxophone for the post-bebop generation. He had taken in the virility of Coleman Hawkins, the swing and airiness of Lester Young, and the progressive ideas of Charlie Parker. Despite a bout of heroin addiction, which he defeated in the mid-1950s, Sonny Rollins had stamina and talent.

114

With Miles Davis, Sonny recorded several of his best-loved songs, such as "Oleo," "Doxy," and "Airegin" (Nigeria spelled backwards.) He played with the group co-led by Clifford Brown and Max Roach. And he achieved recognition for his great performances on recordings led by Thelonious Monk, Art Blakey, Dizzy Gillespie, and Sonny Stitt. He recorded his beautiful and famous Calypso song, "St. Thomas," on his own album. He had a strong, no-nonsense, analytical approach to improvising, and his physical strength was so great that he could play beautifully for an extremely long time. He also began to take chances with harmony, flying high with a modern sense of freedom. He seemed to be a titan—and actually that was not a wrong assessment of him.

But John Coltrane was developing in the late 1950s, playing with Monk and Miles. In 1959, 'Trane formed his own group. He didn't enjoy the immediate success that Rollins had. Earlier in the 1950s, Dizzy, for one, hadn't heard anything special in Coltrane's style. But Miles had. Then Coltrane wanted to stretch out and flex his muscles and test himself. Sonny Rollins might have competed with Coltrane for the title of the greatest saxophonist of their generation. But Sonny dropped out of the running and retreated from the jazz scene for a while. A legend grew up about him when he was seen in the late 1950s practicing on the Brooklyn Bridge.

Sonny would always command respect. But Coltrane's drive, sound, compositional genius, and spiritual quest established him as the more towering figure. Sonny was long winded, but 'Trane stretched upward.

Coltrane made plain his importance with his album *Giant Steps*, named for a song dense with notes and interval leaps. And his "sheets of sound"—the waterfall of notes with which he built his intense compositions—made his music not simply move, but surge. This album also included his blues song, "Cousin Mary," and a tender melody, "Naima," named for his first wife.

In later albums, Coltrane proved that he could also play mellow, standard ballads, and he could explore forcefully. He could play several notes simultaneously on his horn. He would continue that technique in the 1960s when he began to play in the free jazz style.

Born in 1930 in Hamlet, North Carolina, Coltrane grew up in a religious family in High Point. He wended his way up slowly in the jazz world, becoming known first in Miles Davis's quintet in the mid-1950s. His earliest influence had been Charlie Parker. Coltrane had played alto at first but switched to tenor when he decided that he couldn't do anything new or better than Bird had done. On tenor, Coltrane's strongest influences were Lester Young and Coleman Hawkins. He listened carefully to Sonny Rollins, too.

During his years with Davis, Coltrane was addicted to heroin, and he drank too much. After leaving Miles, Coltrane conquered his problems with the help of his wife, Naima, a Moslem. He built a quartet by 1960 that included pianist McCoy Tyner, with his percussive and spiritual approach to music, and the strong, polyrhythmic drummer Elvin Jones. It was another two years before he found a bassist, Jimmy Garrison, who could work with him and play his demanding music.

That year, too, Coltrane fell in love with the Rodgers and Hammerstein tune "My Favorite Things," from the Broadway show *The Sound of Music.* A fan handed him the sheet music. Coltrane also started toying around with the soprano saxophone when a musician left one in the back seat of his car. He had always liked playing some figures in the upper reaches of his tenor. With the new song, the new horn, and a modal approach to improvising, which he had begun working with in Miles's group, 'Trane achieved a distinctive new voice.

He played the song, with its waltz rhythm, in an intense, chanting style, improvising with modes. It became his most popular and commercial success on records. Soon Coltrane was declared the best tenor sax player in *Down Beat* magazine's readers and critics polls, and the soprano saxophone, which he used as his second instrument, developed cachet in the jazz world. Sonny Rollins was no longer the most influential tenor sax man.

Coltrane became caught up in a whirlwind of ideas and influences. Ornette Coleman's free soloing without regard to chords encouraged Coltrane to become more adventurous. Alto saxophonist, bass clarinetist, and flutist Eric Dolphy's great intervallic leaps between registers had a similar effect on Coltrane. He also listened earnestly to the nearly atonal solos of John Gilmore in Sun Ra's Arkestra. These musicians, particularly Dolphy, deserved a great deal of attention. In the modern jazz world, Dolphy's sound, ideas, and technique became beloved by many other musicians.

Indian music was central to 'Trane's development, too. He devised his own scales for improvisation that were, in effect, hybrids of Indian and western modes. The sitar player Ravi Shankar, whom the Beatles would later help popularize in America, went to hear Coltrane in 1961. The two discussed making an album together. The project never materialized. But Coltrane would name one of his sons Ravi in honor of the sitar player. With his close friend Eric Dolphy, John also listened to the music of the African pygmies. They created vocal music of special beauty and intricacy. Books about theory and scales piled up on his living room floor.

In 1961, he recorded with a large ensemble, playing music arranged by Dolphy. Then in one week, during his live engagement at the Village Vanguard, 'Trane did another two albums. "Chasin' the Trane," one of his best performances on a record, contains a sixteen minute solo, and it showed why he was the most exciting horn player of the 1960s. The composition itself, which was very loosely a blues, was improvised on the spot. Its length and scalar style produced a hypnotic effect on listeners. Its tone was searching and urgent. The climax erupted into cries bubbling up over the horn's normal range. Miles asked 'Trane why he played such long songs, and 'Trane replied that it took him all that time to fit in everything he wanted to say.

Not only did he seem to have a bottomless well of stamina and ideas, but he was always impassioned, as a player and as a man—he was always searching. Though he remained a Christian in name all his life, he spent a great deal of time exploring the music and literature of other religions. His overriding interest in spirituality may have begun when his first wife introduced him to the ideas of Islam.

Coltrane was profoundly affected by the bombing of an African-American church in Alabama. Three children were killed there at the height of civil rights activism and demonstrations in the South in 1963. The following June, his friend Eric Dolphy, with whom he had shared so many ideas, died rather suddenly (and very young) in Europe from complications of diabetes.

By that time, Coltrane's marriage to Naima was over. He was involved with another woman, Alice McLeod. She recalled their relationship began with long conversations that convinced her what a "fine person" he was.[1] Alice became his second wife, and the Coltranes began raising a family of three boys and a girl in the early 1960s. From a Baptist church background in Detroit, she immersed herself in 'Trane's spiritual interests and began to play the harp.

In 1964, saddened by the deaths of the Alabama schoolchildren and Dolphy, but buoyed by his relationship with Alice, Coltrane recorded a landmark album, his four-part suite called *A Love Supreme*. The music he composed brought him into close communion with God, he said. Audiences were dazzled and overwhelmed by the four-note motif of "A *Love* Su-*Preme*" and by Coltrane's screams and cries high on the tenor. The incantatory music was based on modes, with strong overtones of Indian philosophical ideas.

Coltrane kept searching for new ways to develop. His album *Ascension*, which was the collective improvisation of eleven players, belongs in the category of free jazz—a style of music in which players improvise off many types of stimuli, not necessarily chords or modes. In this case, the players improvised on four ascending modal scales. Nobody in the group knew anything about the music before arriving at the studio. The musicians were tenor saxophonists Coltrane, Pharaoh Sanders, and Archie Shepp; trumpeters Freddie Hubbard and Dewey Johnson; alto saxophonists Marion Brown and John Tchicai; and rhythm section players. The album was dense with sound.

Critics were astounded by *Ascension* and other such albums, including *Meditations* and *Expression*. The horns screamed intensely. One critic said the music was the most powerful human sound ever heard. Another critic called Pharaoh Sanders amelodic. Sanders, who had loved Sonny Rollins's sound and Coltrane's earlier albums long before he met either musician, paid more attention to Coltrane's sound, phrasing, intonation, tone quality, and whole concept than he did to the critics. "I loved the way he built his solos. He had very well planned ideas," Pharaoh recalled.[2]

In clubs, Coltrane endured criticism for his new music. Some people, including musicians, were moved to exaltation, but others were upset and scandalized by his "overblowing," as they termed his loud, impassioned style, his screams, squeaks, and jagged notes. One club owner in New Jersey asked him to play his old music. He refused, explaining simply that he didn't do that anymore. The club owner insisted, and Coltrane calmly took his group out of the club.

Coltrane was always an intensely serious musician. He was earning a very good income by the mid-1960s, but, unlike Miles, he didn't think about resting or maneuvering for better working conditions. He played ninety-minute sets in clubs and took advantage of the rest periods in between to practice more. At home he practiced the fingering on his horns without blowing on them, so that he wouldn't wake everyone up.

Coltrane's health began to fail. He had a liver ailment, and his drug and alcohol problems in the previous decade had left their mark on him. His exhausting work habits didn't help him. To others, however, he seemed serene. He occupied himself with trying to uplift and encourage people with music. Everyone in jazz felt a profound emptiness and loss when he died in 1967.

Legions of young saxophonists, who copied Coltrane's style, had to struggle to try to establish their own voices on their instruments, so that they wouldn't be labeled as copycats or imitators—especially imitators who simply honked and screamed without really understanding what they were doing. In jazz, originality is one of the highest goals one can aspire to. But so is a knowledge of the tradition, which Coltrane had.

Probably the most individualistic young horn player at this time was Eric Dolphy. He was an experimentalist who worked with many established leaders, but particularly with Charles Mingus, John Coltrane, and Ornette Coleman. Born in 1928, brought up and educated formally in music schools in California, Dolphy became part of the traditional jazz scene in Los Angeles. Virtuosic on the alto saxophone, bass clarinet, and flute, at first he adored Charlie Parker's music.

Multi-reeds player Eric Dolphy, who played with Ornette Coleman, Charles Mingus, and John Coltrane, struggled to achieve public acceptance when atonal-sounding free jazz was in its developmental years in the 1950s and 1960s.

He played with California drummer Chico Hamilton's band in a millionaire's mansion in Newport, Rhode Island, during the 1958 Newport Jazz Festival. New York-based critic Ira Gitler, hearing Dolphy there for the first time, wrote, "Eric's big wide sound filled up the room like the sun that was streaming through the windows." Eric was still playing in a traditional style with Chico.[3]

Then Dolphy moved on to experimenting with "outside" notes. The foundation of his playing was tonal, not chordal in the traditional sense in jazz. He rejected the idea—criticism, actually—that he had left the chords behind. He said that every note in the pieces he played referred to the chords of the pieces he played. That is, they had their own logic.

When Eric came to New York in 1959, he became known for playing experimental music with bassist Charles Mingus's group. "He writes strong, daring music and it's a ball to play with him," Dolphy said about Mingus, who was working on the fringes of "free jazz."

Always short of money, Dolphy moved into trombonist Slide Hampton's house in Brooklyn, where other musicians found some refuge, too. John Coltrane went there to practice with Eric. Freddie Hubbard, who was still trying to play melodic music, felt out of place when he played with Eric. "If [Eric] got a feeling to do something, he would just go ahead and do it. If he was playing a blues and all of a sudden he wanted to [go outside the chords,] he'd do it," Hubbard said.

Among Eric's high-visibility gigs was a concert in 1959 for which he played bass clarinet with Ornette Coleman, a maverick alto saxophonist, at Manhattan's Circle in the Square. Dolphy made some landmark recordings with Mingus's group, led his own groups on records for Prestige, and joined John Coltrane's band by 1961.

Many critics, musicians, and audiences had negative reactions to Eric's music. Because of this, he didn't work enough to earn a decent living. He lived in a loft that let the snow in through the cracks in the walls. He had myriad illnesses. An injury to his leg didn't heal rapidly. He had diabetes but didn't know it. When he won *Down Beat* magazine's New Star award for each of the instruments he played, he wondered if honors meant he would get more work. His tone excited many musicians, even those who didn't like or understand what he was playing. Coltrane helped Dolphy financially. But Eric Dolphy's position in the music business was as precarious as his health.

Throughout the early 1960s, he performed in person and recorded occasionally in the United States and Europe. In 1964, he went to Europe with Mingus's band. Dolphy wanted to see his girlfriend, a dancer, in Paris. He also thought he could get more work in Europe. In a Berlin club, he became sick and was unable to finish the night. A doctor gave him a shot of insulin to bring him out of unconsciousness. The medicine itself or the dose of it was too powerful. Eric died of insulin shock at age thirty-six.

Because he lived at a time when experimental jazz, which everyone called "free jazz," was so controversial, and because he died so young, he never received proper credit for the fiery, exciting ideas he expressed. But his recordings, in particular *The Complete Prestige Recordings of Eric Dolphy*, a nine-CD set issued in 1995, reanimate the musician. Had he lived, he would have found complete acceptance as a great, inventive player and composer by the 1990s. A jazz renaissance was in full bloom, and free jazz sounded far more mellow, entertaining, and comprehensible than it had when Dolphy had struggled to survive.

NINE

ORNETTE COLEMAN, FREE JAZZ, AND JAZZ-ROCK FUSION

Ornette Coleman was another very influential saxophonist in the experimental era. In 1959, this Texas-born alto saxophonist, who had worked on the revolutionary idea of free jazz, took a group into a Greenwich Village club called the Five Spot.

His group's music was totally liberated from the restrictions of chords or any other proscribed musical form. The musicians in his group, including trumpeter Don Cherry, improvised collectively. That is, everyone improvised at the same time, playing different lines in different tempos and keys. Collective improvisation harked back to New Orleans music. Otherwise, free jazz had little in common with any previous style. Free jazz's song structures had nothing to do with the traditional blues or ballads. Essentially, the musicians emphasized sound over form.

Some critics hailed Ornette's cacophonous music as a great innovation for jazz. Others said Ornette Coleman was a strange, destructive force.

Time would prove that Ornette Coleman had latched onto a fascinating, progressive idea. He was actually not the first to start flirting with free jazz. An eccentric keyboardist named Sun Ra explored aspects of free jazz in his Arkestra, and bassist Charles Mingus experimented as well. But Ornette's presentation seemed especially definitive. He upset a great many jazz people. Miles Davis, for one, hated Ornette's work. He said, in effect, that Ornette must be crazy.

But Ornette opened a window wide and let a breeze — or a hurricane, some thought — from a new direction into the jazz world. He was seriously trying to pursue an art music that jazz had inspired him to play. Some people believed he was following the lead of modern European classical composers. And other people thought he was inspired to try something new, to turn the principles of traditional, modern jazz inside out, to call attention to himself. In any case, the modern European composers had a great deal of trouble attracting audiences. Ornette and other free jazz players often met the same sort of resistance.

Ornette's work, which had parallels in the avant-garde compositions and performances of pianist Cecil Taylor and, to a lesser degree, of Charles Mingus and Eric Dolphy, influenced some brilliant, adventurous musicians on all instruments. Among the horn players were trumpeter Don Cherry, who played for Ornette Coleman's surprising debut at the Five Spot. John Coltrane himself was intrigued by Coleman's ideas and became even more daring.

Ornette played a white plastic alto saxophone. He had a highly individual approach to pitch and sound. He ignored the chord progressions, tempo, and phrasing of traditional jazz. In short, he had his own approach to every element of the music.

Gunther Schuller, the noted musician and critic, wrote an article in the *Saturday Review* (January 12, 1957) saying essentially that the form of a song need not come first; the form could evolve out of the material presented. He understood that free jazz had struck upon a valid concept for modern life. But free jazz musicians were starving artists.

Ornette and other free jazz players arrived on the scene at a time when the majority of music fans in the United States were turning to simpler, more elemental rock music. Along with rhythm and blues, soul music, and disco, rock would dominate the popular music world in the 1960s and 1970s.

Many young jazz players were intrigued by Coleman's ideas and compositions. Others who didn't really like the style very much discovered that they had to play it at least some of the time if they wanted to work. Even Birdland featured some avant-garde groups at times. Tradition-rooted pianist Kenny Barron played free jazz there in groups with his older brother, tenor saxophonist Bill. But Birdland closed in the mid-1960s. Its owners had legal problems. Even if they hadn't, the popularity of rock music would probably have forced them to close the club. On the fringes of the American pop music scene, jazz was splintering into stylistic camps.

Throughout the 1960s and 1970s, the avant gardists struggled for survival. They often played in their own lofts for each other's pleasure. Their music couldn't draw audiences who would pay for the pleasure — or ordeal — of hearing musicians struggle with new ideas.

The avant gardists were fiercely protective and supportive of each other. They formed a cult within the jazz world, and some of them said they were making a statement against war, violence, and oppression. To their credit, they had the courage to persist even though the world virtually ignored them and they couldn't earn a living. But because of them, mainstream players began taking risks and chances, and years later their music sounded fresh and not so predictable.

Many horn players with high ideals became involved in the free jazz movement. One of the most interesting groups emerging from the period was the World Saxophone Quartet, formed by multi-reeds player Anthony Braxton, Julius Hemphill, Hamiett Bluiett, a particularly witty baritone saxophonist, and Oliver Lake. They reinterpreted familiar standards such as Duke Ellington's compositions. For audiences who loved the bizarre sound of free jazz ideas, the experiment was a roaring success, and to those who wanted no "improvement" on Ellington, the music sounded eerie.

Ornette Coleman's recordings sparked controversy, but they failed commercially. If the music wasn't always exactly atonal and amelodic, it often sounded that way. Ornette was a celebrated, eccentric cause for much of his career. Usually free jazz, by Coleman and others, was treated as a thing apart from jazz as well as from other American music.

At the same time Coleman was pursuing his ideal, other jazz musicians went in exactly the opposite direction. They began to play jazz/rock fusion. In part it was a reaction against the sad situation in the jazz world. Mainstream musicians playing tradition-rooted music were suffering from poor record sales. Rock musicians were the winners, or at least the breadwinners. They were capturing the imagination of the public and succeeding financially beyond the wildest dreams of most jazz musicians.

In part, rock's elemental beat helped American audiences deal with their feelings of rebellion and escape from their anger and resentment against the political turmoil of the era. President John F. Kennedy, the Reverend Martin Luther King Jr., and Senator Robert F. Kennedy were assassinated. African-American leader Malcolm X, then considered an extremist, was killed, too, because of infighting within the Black Muslim organization. Governor George Wallace, who strongly favored racial segregation in the 1960s, was paralyzed by the bullet of a would-be assassin. And the Vietnam War had divided the nation into two camps: supporters of the war, who believed it was being fought to preserve democracy, and opponents, who didn't trust the government's policy.

Modern jazz, an intellectually demanding music, didn't help Americans to channel their frustrations or vent their anger. The simple melodies and primal beat of rock helped ease the pain. By the end of the 1960s, soul music, an offshoot of rhythm and blues, both mirrored and encouraged the aspirations of African-Americans fighting for integration and equal rights.

It was at this time that Miles Davis recorded *In a Silent Way* and *Bitches Brew*. *Bitches Brew* outstripped all his previous albums in sales. Young people loved it. Nothing about fusion was revolutionary. It didn't add anything to the art of playing any form of music. But it kept elements of jazz before the public. And it spawned new stars who played electric instruments in music circles separate from the jazz and rock worlds.

Among the horn players who crossed over to jazz/rock fusion was fluegelhornist Chuck Mangione. His group had a platinum record— more than a million in sales—with the song "Feels So Good," essentially a pop tune.

The group Weather Report combined rock musicians with leading players from the mainstream jazz world. One of its founders was soprano and tenor saxophonist and composer Wayne Shorter. The group played artistically interesting and commercially appealing music.

In the end, the "free jazz" players were vindicated. Mainstream jazz artists, or artists who straddled the line between mainstream and experimental music, began playing some of Ornette Coleman's compositions. Ornette, who had struggled without commercial success for most of his life, received a MacArthur award, the so-called genius award, in 1995 for his long-standing contribution to jazz.

In the end, free jazz refreshed the work of the mainstream players. By the early 1980s, they were beginning to savor some commercial success again in jazz.

The jazz/rock fusion players were vindicated, too. They loved what they were doing, and the public loved it. Though it often held little fascination for acoustic jazz fans, the genre grew in popularity. And musicians experimented with all the technical equipment at their disposal, producing at times very beautiful and moving music.

TEN

A JAZZ RENAISSANCE

*I*n the late 1970s, rock music concerts were sometimes dangerous; parents didn't want their kids to go to them. And those parents were looking for a more sophisticated form of entertainment. Record companies, noticing a dip in the fortunes of rock, and searching for something to fill the space, reissued some of the great jazz classics in their archives. People of all ages bought the recordings.

Surprised and delighted by this success, the Columbia label decided to take a chance on a new musician — trim, bespectacled trumpeter Wynton Marsalis. When Wynton played in a Lenox, Massachusetts music festival, Gunther Schuller paved the way for him to go to Juilliard. Wynton played both jazz and classical music. On the side, he joined Art Blakey's Jazz Messengers.

Wynton began to favor jazz, which he was then playing in a neo-hard bop, rococo style. Under the influence of Blakey, Wynton was "burning," as jazz people say about someone who is playing exciting sounds. Columbia Records, testing the waters, signed Wynton to make recordings of jazz and classical music. He became successful beyond everyone's wildest dreams — including his own. His albums sold very well. Young women gazed at his posters and declared him adorable. The critics recognized the greatness of his tone and technique.

He left Blakey's group and began performing with his own quintet, including his elder brother, Branford, who plays tenor, baritone, and soprano saxophones. Other record companies, admiring and envious of

Columbia's success with Wynton (and Branford, too), began signing more young players on all the instruments.

In 1982, the Newport Jazz Festival, which had moved to New York City and been renamed the Kool Jazz Festival, started acknowledging the emergence of a new generation of players. One festival concert, called The Young Lions of Jazz, included Wynton Marsalis. Young, new players of the 1960s and 1970s had gone almost unnoticed. They were a neglected, lost generation.

In the 1980s, jazz clubs opened. The venerable old Village Vanguard had lines around the block of people waiting to get in. Club owners discovered that well-known musicians of an earlier generation could attract large crowds. The "lost generation" players developed appeal. True jazz fans knew whom the lost generation masters were.

Among the saxophone players who would get long overdue praise during the renaissance of public interest in jazz were **Gary Bartz, Sonny Fortune,** and free jazz experimenters **David Murray** and **Arthur Blythe,** and trumpeter **Lester Bowie,** who had also been a free jazz explorer. **Lew Tabackin,** co-leader with his wife, Toshiko Akiyoshi, of a prize-winning big band, was a particularly admired saxophonist.

Young musicians flocked to the clubs to try to sit in with the older players and get hired for their groups. The tactic worked, as it had throughout the whole history of jazz. Even a woman saxophonist or trumpeter occasionally got hired; it was a whole new world. Some young players complained that they couldn't get gigs in clubs or lead their own groups. The owners wouldn't take chances on them bringing in listeners. But slowly, everyone's attitude changed. The older generation of jazz musicians was dying. The mid-generation players in their forties and the younger generation in their twenties and thirties kept winning new fans—people who bought recordings and went to clubs and concerts.

Then a technical invention in the late 1980s gave jazz another shot in the arm. Audiences were made up of Yuppies—young, upwardly mobile professionals, who were earning excellent salaries and spending their money on the good life. They bought new electronic equipment, including compact disc players and whatever compact discs were available to put in the machines. Record companies put jazz on CDs. Some people

129

bought jazz without knowing what it was and then fell in love with it.

Wynton Marsalis's family wielded enormous influence in jazz. Wynton's father, Ellis, a pianist, was a prominent teacher in New Orleans. Nearly all his children and protégés seemed to end up with contracts and promising careers. Spike Lee, a young African-American movie maker, hired **Terence Blanchard,** who had studied with Ellis, to write songs and then entire scores.

Alto saxophonists **Steve Coleman** and **Greg Osby,** outside the sphere of the Marsalis family influence, co-led their own group. Coleman helped start an organization with the odd name M-Base in Brooklyn to give young players a chance to hear each other's work and encourage each other in the face of stiff competition. M-Base produced its own concert in a Brooklyn hall. The group split up, in part because the musicians were all building successful careers, going their own ways.

All the while, music schools in cities all across the country kept turning out very accomplished players. In the wake of the Equal Opportunity Acts of the 1960s, the schools had begun hiring veteran jazz musicians to teach youngsters. For example, **Archie Shepp,** an avant-garde horn player, went to teach at the University of Massachusetts.

Talented youngsters studied with jazz and classical professors. The kids developed great technique as players and thoroughly studied the history of jazz, arranging, performing, and composing.

When they competed in awards contests, they astounded the judges. The young musicians played the thrilling old horn solos, which had been improvised by the legendary players in the 1940s, 1950s, and 1960s. Now those older horn players were judging the contests. They laughed with each other after they listened to the kids and their spectacular technique. "They play our solos better than we did originally," they said to each other.

The formerly improvised solos were becoming codified into fixed works of art. At one time, people had worried about the survival of jazz at all. Now people were concerned about the future of experimentation. The future of jazz innovation seemed uncertain in the 1980s and 1990s. Everyone was copying the music of the old masters. But the music that had delighted people with its spontaneity at the moment of its birth in clubs and concert halls was becoming a standard repertory—fixed works of art, like Frédéric Chopin preludes.

130

Jazz was not going to be forgotten or lost. That was a major victory for the art.

Jazz innovation might find its greatest support or most fertile ground in the movies and electronics. Nobody knows for sure. But the survival of the great music of the past is assured in concert halls by the fine young players such as tenor saxophonist *Joshua Redman,* a Harvard graduate who couldn't resist his love of playing jazz. (His father is *Dewey Redman,* an experimenter from the 1960s.)

Alto saxophonists *Bobby Watson* and *Jesse Davis* became major attractions for audiences — Bobby with his beautiful tone and technique, and Davis with his haunting, warm vibrato that recalled the sound of the old masters. *Roy Hargrove, Nicholas Payton, Brian Lynch,* and a few others vied with each other for the title of the greatest young trumpet player of the 1990s. All the while, talented horn players kept coming along in considerable numbers, from every background, race, religion, country — and even both sexes. Until the late 1980s, few women had ever played horns in the front lines in concert halls and famous clubs. *Sue Terry* on saxophones and flute, altoist *Carol Chaikin, Virginia Mayhew* on alto and tenor, trumpeter *Rebecca Coupe Franks,* and trumpeter/ fluegelhornist *Ingrid Jensen* dazzle jazz aficionados.

Club owners in the 1990s often hired young leaders; as a result, few legendary older musicians remained active by then, players like Clark Terry, Harry "Sweets" Edison, Johnny Griffin, Lou Donaldson, Jimmy Heath, James Moody, and Al Grey. A few lesser-known players got the chance to work after spending a lifetime struggling to be heard. Trumpeter *Johnny "Tasty" Parker,* who had toured with swing and blues bands in his teens, substituted in Duke Ellington's band occasionally but lived a completely insecure life. He went from gig to gig in the 1950s, took a government job in the 1960s, and finally landed a steady job as house trumpeter at a popular jazz and disco club in 1977. He was fifty years old when jazz underwent a renaissance. With his sweet tone and pretty ideas, he attracted fans to a sound reflecting a much earlier era, when players like Bobby Hackett and Harold "Shorty" Baker were stars.

Bubba Brooks, an old tenor saxophonist working with the Shorty Jackson Legacy Blues Band in trendy Manhattan restaurants, could bring tears to the eyes of his listeners when he played "Mood Indigo." He had

131

spent years as a journeyman, traveling with rock star Clyde McPhatter's band, then playing club dates around New York. He had a laid-back attitude; some thought that was why the gentlemanly saxophonist, who "played his ass off," as they said, had not become famous with the general public.

Jazz musicians from every generation, playing every style, were finding their niches. If they weren't becoming rich, they were at least finding jobs. Above all, young people, and a dominant number of wind players, were guaranteeing that jazz was alive and well in the clubs and on the bottom lines of the accountants' books.

As mentioned in the Introduction, jazz achieved the reward of its accolade as one of the nation's highest arts by becoming a fixture in Lincoln Center and Carnegie Hall, two of the world's most important cultural organizations. A sweet competition between the two most famous living jazz trumpeters, Jon Faddis and Wynton Marsalis, resolved itself by their cooperation in each other's projects. And the mainstream legacy had prevailed, victorious at the end of jazz's first century.

POSTSCRIPT

There have been many other wonderful horn players not even mentioned in this book, because a complete history would make this book double its length. All the major innovators have been explored here. They guided the history. Among the other significant players are trumpeter Joe Newman, who played for Count Basie; trombonist Britt Woodman in Duke Ellington's band; saxophonists Art Pepper, Louis Jordan, Gene Ammons, Jerry Dodgion, Arnie Lawrence, Pepper Adams, James Spaulding, Oliver Nelson, Clifford Jordan, David "Fathead" Newman, and experimentalist Albert Ayler, and horn players in the bands led by Sun Ra and George Russell. Fluegelhornist/trumpeter Art Farmer and saxophonist Benny Golson led the important Tentet. Clarinetists and saxophonists Eddie Daniels and Ken Peplowski are virtuosos. Saxophonist Joe Henderson has increasingly won much deserved acclaim and popularity. Multi-instrumentalist David Amram is known for his great work with his French horn. And Chico Freeman and young David Sanchez are among the most noteworthy current saxophonists.

SOURCE NOTES

Introduction

1 This quotation has appeared many places.
2 From *The Story of Jazz*, BMG Video, 1994.
3 This and subsequent quotations of Wynton Marsalis are from an interview by the author.
4 From an interview by the author with Roy Hargrove.
5 This and subsequent quotations of Terence Blanchard are from an interview by the author.
6 From an interview by the author with Freddie Hubbard.
7 From interviews with Jon Faddis and Dr. Donald Byrd about a document published by Herbert L. Clarke in the 1920s.
8 From an interview by the author with Vincent Herring.

Chapter One

1 Gary Giddins, *Satchmo* (New York: A Dolphin Book, Doubleday, 1988), p. 26.
2 Leslie Gourse, *Louis' Children: American Jazz Singers* (New York: William Morrow and Company, 1984), p. 23. This and subsequent quotations of Danny Barker are from an interview by the author.
3 Martin Williams, *The Smithsonian Collection of Classic Jazz* (Washington, D.C.: The Smithsonian Collection of Recordings, 1987), p. 9.
4 Giddins, p. 51.

Chapter Two

1 From an interview by the author with Doc Cheatham.
2 From an interview by the author with Jonah Jones.
3 Gunther Schuller, *Early Jazz* (London: Oxford University Press, 1968), pp. 138–139 ff., and Rudolph Blesh, *Shining Trumpets: A History of Jazz* (New York, Da Capo Press,

1976; originally published in 1946), p. 199; both cited in Len Lyons, *The 101 Best Jazz Albums* (New York: William Morrow and Company, 1980), p. 76.
4 From an interview by the author with Peanuts Hucko.
5 From "Louis Armstrong: A Self-Portrait," edited by Richard Meryman, *Life* magazine, April 15, 1966 (reprinted by Eakins Press, New York, 1971). The quotations can be found in Leslie Gourse, *Louis' Children: American Jazz Singers* (New York: William Morrow and Co., 1984), pp. 28–29.
6 From an interview by the author with Peanuts Hucko.
7 "Louis Armstrong: A Self-Portrait." The quotation can be found in Leslie Gourse, *Louis' Children*, p. 29.
8 Leslie Gourse, *Louis' Children*, p. 32.

Chapter Three

1 Ira Gitler, *Swing To Bop* (New York: Oxford University Press, 1985), p. 47.
2 *Piano Jazz*, with Marian McPartland, host, and Roy Eldridge, August 18, 1986, National Public Radio, available on a Jazz Alliance compact disc.
3 A very good example of his piano playing and his ineffable charm was recorded when he was a guest of pianist Marian McPartland on her National Public Radio show, "Piano Jazz." Roy played and sang his French composition. A CD of the show was released on the Jazz Alliance label in 1995.

Chapter Four

1 Leslie Gourse, *Louis' Children: American Jazz Singers* (New York: William Morrow and Company, 1984), p. 146.

2 George T. Simon, *The Big Bands* (New York: Schirmer Books, 1971), p. 85.

3 Simon, p. 294.

Chapter Five

1 Dizzy Gillespie with Al Fraser, *To Be Or Not To Bop* (Garden City, N.Y.: Doubleday and Company, 1979), p. 114.

2 WKCR-FM, fiftieth anniversary celebration of Dizzy's recording career, 1987, hosted by Phil Schaap. Subsequent quotations of Dizzy Gillespie are from this source unless otherwise noted.

3 Ira Gitler, *Jazz Masters of the 40s* (New York: Macmillan, 1966, reprinted Da Capo, New York, 1983), p. 26.

4 From an interview by the author with Dizzy Gillespie.

5 Gillespie and Fraser, p. 192, and also in an interview by the author with Gil Fuller.

6 From a conversation between Lorraine Gillespie and the author.

7 Liner notes for *Max Plus Diz* in Paris, 1989, a two-CD set, A&M Records.

8 Gillespie and Fraser, p. 249.

9 Len Lyons, *The 101 Best Jazz Albums* (New York: William Morrow and Company, 1980), p. 174.

10 Gillespie and Fraser, p. 393.

Chapter Six

1 From an interview by the author with Anita Evans.

2 "The Miles Davis Project," narrated by Danny Glover, produced by the American Radio Network, aired on WNYC-FM in 1995. Subsequent quotations of Miles Davis are from this source.

Chapter Eight

1 From an interview by the author with Alice McLeod Coltrane.

2 From an interview by the author with Pharaoh Sanders.

3 Liner notes for *The Complete Prestige Recordings of Eric Dolphy*. Subsequent quotations are from this source.

SUGGESTED LISTENING

Because many great horn players can be heard together in bands and small groups, I have sometimes recommended one recording including several players at once. If I were to include recordings by all the great horn players who should be mentioned, this list would be virtually endless. I have listed recordings primarily for innovative and key players.

This list is based to a great degree on the compact discs available in record stores at the end of 1996. Often the recordings for which horn players became famous are no longer available in the form in which they were originally released, and they have been reorganized and reissued under new titles or within collections.

Many of the great horn players can also be heard on recordings available in the "Smithsonian Collection of Classic Jazz." The collection can be purchased from the Smithsonian Institution, Washington, D.C. 20560.

For some horn players, only one or two CDs have been listed here, but there are often many exemplary albums, as in the cases of Dizzy Gillespie and Charlie "Bird" Parker. And for some players, no specific album with label and release date has been listed, but albums for which they are particularly known have been included. You can go to record stores and browse through the bins, looking for the recordings—usually collections on CDs—that correspond to the information in this book; for example, in the record store section for tenor saxophonist Coleman Hawkins, look for any CD that includes his 1939 recording of "Body and Soul." He recorded that song many times, but the 1939 version is regarded as the classic one. That recording happens to be included here on a CD.

In cities with record stores specializing in "golden oldies" for collectors, you may be able to find the original 78- or 33-rpm records.

As much as possible, this list proceeds in chronological order, based on the years the horn players emerged as stars. The dates listed for the recordings signify the reissue dates for the CDs. Sometimes the original recording dates are noted, too.

Louis Armstrong, *Greatest Hot Fives and Sevens*, Living Era label, 1995, includes his classic first recording of "West End Blues"; *Portrait of the Artist as a Young Man*, 1923–1934, Columbia.

Bix Beiderbecke and the Wolverines, originally recorded in 1925, Timeless, 1993; *The Complete Bix Beiderbecke*, with Frankie Trumbauer and the Paul Whiteman Band, IRD Records, 1991.

Jabbo Smith's Rhythm Aces, 1929–1938, Classics label.

Henry "Red" Allen Collection, Vols. 1–4, Collectors Classics label.

Jack Teagarden and His Orchestra, 1939–40, and *1934– 39* (two different CDs), Classics label, 1993.

Duke Ellington's orchestras included many of the great horn players:

Duke Ellington & His Famous Orchestra, Folklore, originally recorded in 1941, includes Rex Stewart, Ray Nance, Lawrence Brown, Sam Nanton, Juan Tizol, Otto Hardwicke, Johnny Hodges, Barney Bigard, Ben Webster, and Harry Carney. Recorded later, *The Best of Duke Ellington*, reissued on Pablo, 1980, and again by Fantasy, 1991, has Clark Terry, Jimmy Owens, Quentin "Butter" Jackson, Paul Gonsalves, Jimmy Hamilton, Russell Procope, Cootie Williams, Norris Turney, Britt Woodman, Cat Anderson, Shorty Baker, and Harold Ashby.

Benny Carter Songbook, Music Masters Jazz, 1996, with a variety of singers, contains two of his classic compositions, "Key Largo" and "When Lights Are Low"; *Benny Carter, 1928–1952*, RCA, 1979 (two discs).

Coleman Hawkins Greatest Hits, includes the version of "Body and Soul" originally done in 1939, BMG.

Roy Eldridge/Coleman Hawkins, on Stash, is a collaboration between these two great players who worked together often; Roy Eldridge, *Uptown*, has classic recordings done with drummer Gene Krupa and singer Anita O'Day, Columbia.

Benny Goodman's bands included many great horn players. The album *This Is Jazz* has Harry James and others and contains the song "Sing Sing Sing"; *Benny Goodman: Live at Carnegie Hall*, the landmark jazz concert that took place on January 16, 1938, including trumpeters Harry James, Ziggy Elman, Pee Wee Erwin, Bunny Berigan, and Buck Clayton and saxophonistsis Lester Young, Johnny Hodges, and Harry Carney, is on Columbia.

Count Basie's bands contained some of the greatest horn players in the 1930s, 1940s, and 1950s. One of them was tenor saxophonist Lester Young, who recorded with Basie on *Blue Lester*, Savoy, and on *Lester Leaps In*, Living Era, reissued in 1995. Lester Young was in Basie's early band, along with trumpeters Buck Clayton and Harry "Sweets" Edison, saxophonists Herschel Evans and Earl Warren, and trombonist Dickie Wells. Later bands included saxophonists Frank Wess, Frank Foster, Eddie "Lockjaw" Davis, and Marshall Royal, trombonist Benny Powell, and trumpeter Thad Jones. Some of the albums are *Count Basie and His Orchestra, 1940–41*, with Coleman Hawkins, Buck Clayton, tenor saxophonists Don Byas and Buddy Tate, and Sweets Edison, Classic Records, 1991; *Count Basie and His Orchestra: Jumpin' at the Woodside, 1937–43*, and *Count Basie: Jumpin' at the Woodside*, Vol. 2, recorded 1955–1959, both on Jazz Roots label.

Dizzy Gillespie: The bins are filled with CDs by Dizzy Gillespie on many labels. His most important work begins in the mid-1940s. Dizzy Gillespie and Charlie Parker, *Jazz at Massey Hall*, Original Jazz Classics, done originally for the Debut label in 1953, was referred to as "The Greatest Jazz Concert Ever." Many other albums are by Dizzy and Bird together, or separately leading their own groups. Among them are bebop recordings done in February and May 1945, including the songs "Groovin' High," "Dizzy Atmosphere," "All the Things You Are," "Shaw Nuff," "Lover Man," the great classic "Salt Peanuts," and "Hot House." *The Complete RCA Victor Recordings* has a sampling of Gillespie's playing from 1937 to 1949, including the Metronome All Stars on January 3, 1949, with Miles Davis and Fats Navarro on trumpet, Kai Winding and J. J. Johnson on trombone, Buddy DeFranco on clarinet, Charlie Parker on alto sax, and Charlie Ventura on tenor sax.

Charlie "Bird" Parker: Bird's recordings for Savoy and on Dial, to name a portion of his work, are masterpieces. For the romantically inclined, his recordings with strings on Verve are required listening. Some CDs now available are *The Cole Porter Song Book,* Verve, 1991; *Charlie Parker with Strings — The Master Takes,* Verve, 1995; *Jazz at the Philharmonic,* recorded 1946, reissued on Verve, 1992; *Bird: The Complete Charlie Parker on Verve; Bird and Diz,* with pianist Thelonious Monk, bassist Curly Russell, and drummer Buddy Rich, Verve, recorded 1950, reissued on Polygram, 1986; *Young Bird,* Vol. 3, 1945, including the songs "Salt Peanuts," "Shaw Nuff," "Lover Man," and "Hot House." On at least one CD on Verve is a recommended recording of a little blues called "Au Privave."

Tommy Dorsey, himself a fine trombonist, led bands including trumpeter Charlie Shavers and clarinetist Buddy DeFranco.

Within singer and clarinetist Woody Herman's band, the Four Brothers, tenor saxophonists Zoot Sims, Stan Getz, and Herbie

Stewart and baritone saxophonist Serge Chaloff distinguished themselves as a progressive group. Later Al Cohn and Gene Ammons played in the group.

Baritone saxophonist Gerry Mulligan led a pianoless quartet including trumpeter Chet Baker, recordings on the Pacifica Jazz label. *The Best of Chet Baker,* Pacifica Jazz, 1953–1956, reissued by Capitol, 1989, is a good example of the Mulligan sideman who rose to become a star in his own right.

Tenor saxophonists John Coltrane and Johnny Griffin recorded with pianist Thelonious Monk live at the Five Spot Café in New York City in 1957 and 1958 respectively. Coltrane's CD, on the Blue Note label, was released in 1993, and Griffin's recording was on the Riverside label in 1958. Tenor saxophonist Charlie Rouse recorded with Monk for the Columbia label throughout the 1960s.

Miles Davis: Recommended are any or all of his albums from the late 1950s through the 1960s, such as *Porgy and Bess, ESP, In a Silent Way, Miles Ahead (Miles + 19), Milestones, Miles Smiles, Sorcerer,* with Wayne Shorter on tenor saxophone, *Miles Davis — The Complete Concert, 1964 + Four and More* at Philharmonic Hall, including tenor saxophonist George Coleman, and *Stella By Starlight,* including Coleman and Cannonball Adderley, all on Columbia reissues in the 1990s.

Clifford Brown, containing the first and last of his recorded performances, was a 1973 Columbia release now on CD. Also, several CDs co-led by Clifford Brown and drummer Max Roach in the mid-1950s are now available.

Stan Getz, *Getz/Gilberto,* featuring Antonio Carlos Jobim and Astrud Gilberto with Getz and Joao Gilberto, has the hit songs "The Girl from Ipanema," "Desafinado,"

137

and "Corcovado," among others, Verve, 1964; *Bossa Nova*, Verve, 1962.

Paul Desmond, *Jazz Impressions of Eurasia*, in group led by pianist Dave Brubeck, Columbia, 1992.

Dexter Gordon, *Dexter Calling*, Blue Note, 1961, reissued 1987. Also available are recordings by Dexter done with leading European players in Copenhagen, Denmark.

Julian "Cannonball" Adderley, *Cannonball in Japan*, including "Work Song" and "Mercy, Mercy, Mercy," Capitol, 1990.

Sonny Rollins, *Saxophone Colossus*, DCC Jazz, 1956.

John Coltrane, *Giant Steps*, 1960, and *My Favorite Things*, 1961, both on Atlantic, are two of his most famous albums, featuring him on tenor and soprano saxophones.

Ornette Coleman, *The Shape of Jazz To Come*, with his original quartet (Don Cherry on cornet, Charlie Haden on bass, and Billy Higgins on drums), Atlantic, 1959.

Eric Dolphy, *At the Five Spot*, Vols. 1 and 2,

Prestige. Also recommended are his recordings led by bassist Charles Mingus.

Thad Jones: Among the available CDs in the bins at the end of 1996, none were with his band, the Jones-Lewis Orchestra. A collection of that band's work is available, however, from Mosaic Records, Stamford, Connecticut.

John Surman, *The Amazing Adventures of Simon Simon*, ECM Records, 1981.

Steve Turre, *Sanctified Shells*, Antilles, 1993.

Bobby Watson, *Enja*, 1995. Any album by this young master of the alto saxophone is recommended.

Wynton Marsalis, recordings on Columbia label. Choose any of this virtuoso's CDs.

The exciting modern trumpeter Jerry Gonzalez has his own Fort Apache band on CDs. Other young trumpeters, such as Terence Blanchard, Roy Hargrove, and Nicholas Payton, have many albums in the bins, and Blanchard is also the composer for movie soundtracks such as *Malcolm X*.

These players are representative of the great horn players in jazz history. For more, refer to the Tree in the middle of this book and browse through the bins to choose albums that appeal to you.

Drummer Art Blakey was noted for the great horn players in his group, the Jazz Messengers, such as Bobby Watson and Branford Marsalis on alto sax and Wynton Marsalis and Terence Blanchard on trumpet.

The Carnegie Hall Jazz Band, led by trumpeter Jon Faddis, and the Lincoln Center Jazz Orchestra, led by trumpeter Wynton Marsalis, both with many great young players and some experienced veterans of the big bands, now have CDs available.

If any albums by the group Sphere are available, its tenor saxophonist, Charlie Rouse, is especially notable. Cedar Walton's CD *Composer*, on Astor Place Records, 1996, includes alto saxophonist Vincent Herring, tenor saxophonist Ralph Moore, and trumpeter Roy Hargrove.

FOR FURTHER READING

Music magazines often publish stories on classic and contemporary singers. Among the magazines that can be found on newsstands and in music libraries are *Down Beat, Jazz Times, Jazz Iz*, and *Musician*.

Armstrong, Louis. *My Life in New Orleans*. Englewood Cliffs, N.J.: Prentice Hall, 1954. Reprinted by Da Capo Press, New York, 1986.

Benny, King of Swing. New York: Thames and Hudson, 1979. Reprinted by Da Capo Press, New York, 1987. A pictorial biography based on Benny Goodman's archives.

Britt, Stan. *Dexter Gordon*. New York: Da Capo Press, 1989. The tenor saxophonist's life story, told by a British jazz writer. Originally published by Quartet in London.

Cheatham, Adolphus "Doc." *I Guess I'll Get the Papers and Go Home*. London: Cassell, 1995. The life of the trumpeter who began playing trumpet and saxophone professionally in the 1920s, became a star in his seventies, and kept going into his nineties.

Chilton, John. *Sidney Bechet: The Wizard of Jazz*. New York: Oxford University Press, 1987. A biography of the New Orleans-born soprano saxophonist, who became a legend best known in Europe.

———. *The Song of the Hawk*. Ann Arbor: University of Michigan Press, 1980. A biography of Coleman Hawkins by the highly respected British saxophonist and jazz writer.

Davis, Miles, with Quincy Troupe. *Miles: The Autobiography*. New York: Simon & Schuster, 1989. Miles gives his candid, sometimes shockingly profane appraisal of his world and colleagues.

Down Beat: 60 Years of Jazz. Milwaukee, Wis.: Hal Leonard Corporation, 1995. A collection of articles dating from the 1930s into the 1990s reprinted from the historic jazz magazine. Subjects include Benny Goodman, Bunny Berigan, Louis Armstrong, Dizzy Gillespie, Charlie Parker, Roy Eldridge, Miles Davis, Lester Young, Clifford Brown, Sonny Rollins, John Coltrane, Ornette Coleman, Coleman Hawkins, Jack Teagarden, Lee Morgan, J. J. Johnson, Dexter Gordon, Thad Jones, Benny Carter, Branford Marsalis, Joe Henderson, Greg Osby, and Anthony Braxton.

Giddins, Gary. *Celebrating Bird: The Triumph of Charlie Parker*. New York: Beech Tree Books, 1987. This insightful book by a leading jazz critic is very nicely illustrated.

———. *Rhythm-A-Ning*. New York: Oxford University Press, 1985. A collection of essays about horn players James Moody, Sonny Stitt, Lester Young, Roy Eldridge, Arthur Blythe, Pee Wee Erwin, Illinois Jacquet, Stan Getz, Ornette Coleman, Wynton Marsalis and others.

Gillespie, Dizzy, with Al Fraser. *To Be Or Not To Bop*. Garden City, N.Y.: Doubleday and

Company, 1979. Dizzy talks about his ribald life and high-minded philosophy and musical endeavors and achievements.

Gitler, Ira. *Jazz Masters of the 1940s*. New York: Macmillan, 1966. Includes articles and essays on Charlie Parker and the alto and baritone saxophonists, Dizzy Gillespie and the trumpeters, J. J. Johnson and the trombonists, and Dexter Gordon and the tenor saxophonists.

Goldberg, Joe. *Jazz Masters of the 1950s*. New York: Macmillan, 1965. Includes articles on Gerry Mulligan, Miles Davis, Sonny Rollins, Paul Desmond, John Coltrane, and Ornette Coleman.

Gordon, Max. *Live from the Village Vanguard*. New York: St. Martin's Press, 1980. A collection of the club owner's intimate views of Sonny Rollins, Rahsaan Roland Kirk, and Thad Jones and his jazz orchestra's trip to Russia.

Gourse, Leslie. *Dizzy Gillespie and the Birth of Bebop*. New York: Atheneum, 1994. Dizzy's life story, including his relationship with Charlie Parker.

Hadlock, Richard. *Jazz Masters of the 1920s*. New York: Macmillan, 1972. Articles and essays about Louis Armstrong, Bix Beiderbecke, Jack Teagarden, and others.

Jones, Max. *Talking Jazz*. New York: W. W. Norton, 1988. A collection of articles by a leading British jazz writer, who was a regular contributor to the *Melody Maker* magazine in London. His subjects include such historic figures as clarinetist Barney Bigard, saxophonists Stan Getz, Johnny Griffin, Coleman Hawkins, Johnny Hodges, Gerry Mulligan, Flip Phillips, Zoot Sims, Lucky Thompson, and Ben Webster, and trumpeters Red Allen, Buck Clayton, Harry "Sweets" Edison, and Jonah Jones.

Lindemeyer, Paul. *Celebrating the Saxophone*. New York: Hearst Books, 1996. A beautifully illustrated history of the instrument.

Maggin, Donald L. *Stan Getz: A Life in Jazz*. New York: William Morrow and Company, 1996.

Marsalis, Wynton. *Marsalis on Music*. New York: W. W. Norton, 1995.

Meryman, Richard. *Louis Armstrong: A Self-Portrait*. New York: Eakins Press, 1971.

Pepper, Art and Laurie. *Straight Life: The Story of Art Pepper*. New York: Schirmer Books, 1979. The saxophonist's adventures in music and battles with drugs.

Porter, Lewis, ed. *A Lester Young Reader*. Washington, D.C.: Smithsonian Institution Press, 1992. A variety of articles and personal interviews by some of the foremost jazz writers.

Simon, George T. *The Big Bands*. New York: Schirmer Books, 1967. Provides a wealth of information about the great and historic jazz horn players.

Spellman, A. B. *Four Lives in the Bebop Business*. New York: Limelight Editions, 1985. Two of the four musicians are saxophonists Ornette Coleman and Jackie McLean.

Stewart, Rex. *Jazz Masters of the 1930s*. New York: Macmillan, 1972. Stewart, who played with Duke Ellington, gives a musician's wonderfully written view of the jazz world, with stories about Louis Armstrong, Tricky Sam Nanton, Barney Bigard, Ben Webster, Harry Carney, Benny Carter, and others.

Wilmer, Valerie. *Jazz People*. London: Allison & Busby, 1977. This book is a collection of articles and essays on such horn players as fluegelhornists and trumpeters Art Farmer and Clark Terry, trumpeters Buck Clayton and Howard McGhee, tenor saxophonists Eddie "Lockjaw" Davis, Jimmy Heath, and Archie Shepp, and alto saxophonist Jackie McLean.

INDEX

Page numbers in *italics* refer to photographs. Principal references to musicians appear in **boldface**.

DATE DUE

APR 9 '04			
GAYLORD			PRINTED IN U.S.A.